The Pastor as Theologian

PASTORAL MINISTRY SERIES

(A series for pastors and laypeople, which addresses the nature
and scope of ministry as a task of the congregation)

The Pastor as Theologian

EDITED BY

Earl E. Shelp
and
Ronald H. Sunderland

The Pilgrim Press

NEW YORK

Copyright © 1988 The Pilgrim Press

All rights reserved

The biblical quotations in this book are, unless otherwise indicated, from the *Revised Standard Version of the Bible,* copyright 1946, 1952, and © 1971, 1973 by the Division of Christian Education, National Council of Churches, and are used by permission. Excerpts marked NEB are from *The New English Bible,* © The Delegates of the Oxford University Press and the Syndics of the Cambridge University Press 1961, 1970, and are reprinted with permission. The quotations marked KJV are from the *King James Version.*

Library of Congress Cataloging-in Publication Data

The Pastor as theologian.
  (Pastoral ministry series)
  "Originally presented as the Parker memorial lectures in theology and ministry at the Institute of Religion in Houston during the spring of 1987"—Acknowledgments.
  Bibliography: p. 130
  1. Pastoral theology. I. Shelp, Earl E., 1947–
II. Sunderland, Ronald, 1929– . III. Title: Parker memorial lectures in theology and ministry.
IV. Series.
BV4017.P27   1988   253   88-9077
ISBN 0-8298-0776-4

The Pilgrim Press, 132 West 31 Street, New York, NY 10001

Contents

Acknowledgments

The essays contained in this volume were originally presented as the Parker Memorial Lectures in Theology and Ministry at the Institute of Religion in Houston during the spring of 1987. A sixth lecture was presented by Dr. Sandra R. Brown, but for reasons beyond her control her essay regrettably is not included in this book.

Funding for this fourth annual series of lectures was provided in loving memory of R.A. (Al) Parker by a donor who wishes not to be identified. Mr. Parker was a dedicated and enthusiastic trustee of the Institute of Religion. His contribution to the ministries of the Institute of Religion and to the life of the church is perpetuated through the publication of this volume and the preceding volumes in the "Pastoral Ministry Series." The financial generosity of the person who underwrote these lectures is gratefully acknowledged.

Appreciation also is expressed to J. Robert Nelson, Director of the Institute of Religion, and to the Trustees of the Institute of Religion for their important, supportive contribution to the annual lectures and consequent publication. All the lecturers orally presented their ideas clearly and informatively, and the written versions included here reflect a similar clarity and helpful insight regarding an important subject. Juanita Veasey assisted in preparing the typescripts for publication, and Marion M. Meyer of The Pilgrim Press performed her annual magic act of transforming manuscripts into a book. To each and all, the editors express appreciation.

The Pastor as Theologian

Introduction

Earl E. Shelp and Ronald H. Sunderland

THE ROLES OF PASTOR AND THEOLOGIAN OFTEN ARE PER-
ceived in the life of the church to be separate and distinct.
Laypeople understand the pastor role to be parish based
and practical in its emphasis, whereas the theologian role is
understood to be in higher education and concerned more
with abstract ideas than with living the faith. This perception, in fact, may be fostered not only by the physical
settings in which pastors and theologians labor, but also by
the self-understandings or self-descriptions of the people in
each role. Pastors may give priority to person-to-person
ministry, budgeting little time or having little inclination
for cognitive activities that are not seen as immediately
relevant to the numerous programs of congregations. Theo-

Earl E. Shelp, Ph.D., is Research Fellow, Institute of Religion, and Assistant Professor of Medical Ethics, Baylor College of Medicine, Houston.

Ronald H. Sunderland, Ed.D., is Research Fellow, Institute of Religion,
Houston.

1

logians may sense a priority to equip church leaders through teaching and through clarifying and validating reasoning about Christian faith. Pastors and theologians, as a consequence, may share a commitment to the faith and their respective work, but may fail to appreciate fully the organic and interdependent relationship of their respective activities.

The contributors to this volume critically examine the roles and tasks of pastors and theologians, addressing, in particular, the importance of pastors being theologians and doing the work of theologians. From their several perspectives, each argues that the estrangement between pastor and theologian is artificial. They collectively offer a corrective to this state of affairs by demonstrating the organic and interdependent relationship of theology, worship, mission, and discipleship. Speaking primarily to pastors, the authors argue that "pastoring" without concern for or drawing on the resources of the intellectual discipline of theology impoverishes pastoral ministry. Similarly, they argue that "theologizing" without concern for or drawing on the experiences and needs of people in congregations impoverishes theological scholarship.

This book, like others in the series,[1] is intended to clarify our understanding of the multiple facets or aspects of pastoral ministry as a function of lay and ordained people. It is intended to encourage the people of God, especially pastors, to give appropriate attention to this foundational and characteristic theological dimension of Christian identity and activity. More specifically, because they are envisaged as the principal readers, pastors are reminded that they can be a crucial integrating factor that brings doctrine and discipleship into contact and dialogue. Thus the parish and academy can be brought together in the person and ministry of a pastor who facilitates a constructive enterprise of inquiry, interpretation, and application. Pastors, it seems, are strategically situated in and through their ministries to call on the past, address the present, and equip for the future as they minister to people and test distinct beliefs and perspectives in the light of contemporary events and experiences.[2]

Pastors *and* theologians work within a context of Christian tradition and the authority claimed by and for it. Each is involved in testing that tradition and authority, but perhaps in differing ways. Each is aware of how cognitive, sociopolitical, and cultural factors bear on tradition and authority. Each is aware of the challenges and influences of non-Christian and divergent Christian beliefs on understandings of truth and the life of faith. Pastors understand these factors as components of daily life with which they interact. Theologians understand these as formative factors of theology. As such, pastors and theologians are engaged in a common work of testing, refining, and applying theology in relevant and meaningful ways to new situations, utilizing the language of the culture within which each lives while concurrently seeking to be consistent with the whole, developing Christian understanding. In order for the pastor and the theologian to perform their tasks competently, each ought to be aware of the resources available from the other and to be sensitive to the distinct concerns of the other. They share a common interest in Christian faith that understands theology as a pivotal, continuous activity in which basic concepts and beliefs are tested, reformulated, and transmitted to meet new conditions and challenges.[3] This commonality and the contribution that pastors can make to theology, as well as the contribution that theology can make to pastors, are examined in the following essays.

Albert Outler explores the relationship of theology to the

3

pastoral office and to pastoral practice. He understands "pastor" in the traditional sense of a devoted caretaker of a people, noting, however, that understandings of the pastoral role change over time. Given these changes, there is a need for every generation to clarify its understanding of pastor, which has as a key characteristic a conviction that meaning is grounded in God. Pastoral caretaking, accordingly, is based in this conviction and in a commitment to God's rule and God's righteousness. By understanding and acting on these beliefs, the "sheep" are fed.

Outler argues that a "good" pastor has a primary concern for people and engages in "sense-making talk about God." "Sense-making talk about God" makes a pastor a theologian. It awakens people's sense of the sacred and conveys its import for living. In order to perform this function, pastors should be teachers or guides and midwives to insight and inquiry. He acknowledges that pastors do not need to be a theologian's theologian to fill this role or meet this need. They properly and unembarrassingly can be "folk-theologians," instructing people about God's gracious and upholding presence. Finally, according to Outler, "sense-making talk about God" will involve "good" pastors in addressing God in prayer, praise, and communion.

Gayraud Wilmore's essay illustrates the importance of experiences to theology, and thus the crucial role of pastoral ministry to the theological enterprise. Wilmore understands theology as a human way of thinking and talking about God out of a particular context. In his opinion, all theologies reflect the experience, in its broadest sense, of a person or a people. With respect to the experience of black theology, its distinctiveness arises from the experience of black people, which leads to a theology that is eminently pastoral—linking the pastor's study to events in the streets, linking prayer to political action, and linking the history of a people to a theology for all people. The experience of a people refracted through the light of the gospel, according to Wilmore, becomes the raw materials for fashioning a theology. A theology of this sort is pastoral, addressing people in life situations. Survival, education, and liberation thus become themes of black theology, and the spiritual and pastoral are joined.

According to this understanding, piety and practical action are inseparable. The congregation and its activities in worship and education set the spiritual context for the congregation's mission in the world. The mission is, in part, in response to every inauthentic and unauthorized power over people's lives, as determined by the standard of the gospel. The evolution of black theology, with its strongly pastoral character, Wilmore argues, challenges other theologies to be faithful to the gospel, grounded in the lives of people whose experience of the world includes suffering and powerlessness. At this point there is a common experience that renders irrelevant any and all other identifying or segregating characteristics. Thus Wilmore concludes that even though black theology is a theology reflective of a particular context and experience of a people, it expresses a universal message and constitutes a call for Christian solidarity.

The third essay, by Will Campbell, discusses theological preaching. Campbell claims that authentic theological preaching speaks more in terms of faith than in terms of certainty. But he observes that contemporary theological preaching tends to defend the latter rather than to confess the former. By so doing theological preaching leads to violence as disputes emerge and are coercively settled. Campbell argues against this trend by suggesting that theological preaching properly is a cautious enterprise, talking about God and applying beliefs about God to life. Defending or espousing doctrine, according to Campbell, is not what Jesus did, but what churches and church leaders seem prone to do. If Jesus is the model, then these contemporary deviations are suspect. For Campbell, the substance of theological preaching ought not to be defending or espousing doctrine. Rather, theological preaching consists in living, not only proclaiming, a life of faith in community.

The discussion of preaching and theology is extended in the essay by David Read. Read offers two reasons why contemporary sermons seem to lack theological content. First, he suggests that the pace of activities and programs in a parish distract pastors from the necessary commitment of time to bridge the worlds of theological study and pastoral practice. Second, he proposes that theologians may have little experience in the parish, and thus may be out of touch with the realities or contingencies of daily life that often concern parishioners and pastors. Nevertheless Read defends the relative independence of scholars to pursue certain studies for their intrinsic merit without necessarily measuring a theologian's competence by the proficiency of the preaching (content or style) of his or her students.

Speaking as a pastor to academic theologians, Read argues that the academic discipline of theology and the discipline of preparing people for ministry or preaching should be seen as related and complementary. On the one hand, preachers should acknowledge the importance of and their dependence on theology. On the other hand, theologians should be sensitive to the needs of the church for effective preachers and should be part of the life of a congregation. In short, Read calls for more contact and discussion between theologians and pastors/preachers. He speaks additionally to theologians/professors, encouraging them to recognize that they have a pastoral or nurturing obligation to students and that they should help students to examine the content of faith and to be effective communicators and interpreters of that faith. Pastors, alternately, have a teaching obligation to professors: reminding them to make their knowledge intelligible to laypeople.

Read concludes by addressing pastors, calling attention to their obligation to preach sermons with theological content. Pastors should be appreciative of the work of theologians, looking to them for guidance and inspiration. Alternatively, theologians and seminaries should be mindful of the total life of the church as they define either role and decide how to fulfill it. Read ends his analysis of "what pastors can teach theologians" with a call for a deeper sense of unity among the manifestations of the church, asking theologians to be active in the total life of the church.

In the concluding essay Max Stackhouse examines pastoral ministry to the world outside the church. His discussion of "The Pastor as Public Theologian" begins with an observation that the pastoral virtues of faith, hope, and love are rooted in the grace of God. These virtues plus wisdom are considered by Stackhouse to be indispensable to pastoral ministries undertaken within congregational life. He argues, however, that there is a public world of secular institutions that is a larger context for ministry. Ministry in this larger context requires a public theology to undergird it. A public theology, according to Stackhouse, represents what ultimately is theologically true about life and just in life. Thus pastors are seen to have a mission to be a philosophical-theologian, equipping all people (people of faith and people of no faith) to discern revelations of God's truth and justice in the world. This task or mission may appear beyond the reach of pastors, but Stackhouse argues that it cannot and must not be ignored, despite the difficulties associated with it. A public theology, which he considers crucial, provides a foundation for common life and criteria by which the conduct of common life is judged. A public theology articulates a metaphysical-moral vision that grounds and guides civilization. As such, it is indispensable, since it recovers and recasts basic notions of truth and justice for public consideration. The mission of pastors, accordingly, is not only to help congregants learn about truth and justice, but to help public and social institutions as well. By so doing the pastoral mission, undergirded by a public theology, is directed toward the salvation of individuals and civilizations.

Several themes emerge from these diverse but rich analyses of the interrelatedness of pastor, pastoral ministry, and theology. These themes help to clarify and broaden our perception of the pastoral office, pastoral activity, and its theological foundation. Five key concerns are presented as central to the total discussion. First, the organic relationship between pastoral ministry and the discipline of theology ought to be acknowledged. Each role and function needs and can learn from the other. The two roles within the church are interdependent and complementary. The pastoral office gains its distinctiveness from its theological source, and theologians must be aware of how their work serves the needs of the church. Second, thinking about God (theology) and applying beliefs about God to life (mission, worship, and discipleship) are both activities of faith. In theological preaching they are united in talk about living a life of faith in community, not in articulating and defending doctrine. Third, pastoral ministry, when properly understood theologically, considers the world outside the church also as a congregation to which ministry is offered. As such, pastors are theologians of the church and public theologians articulating a metaphysical-moral vision of what is true about life and just in life, thus providing a theologial foundation and guide for common life. Fourth, pastors, as devoted caretakers of a people, ought to engage in "sense-making talk about God." By so doing a pastor is a theologian instructing people about God's gracious, upholding presence and guiding people to God in prayer, praise, and communion. Fifth, the theological foundation and identity of pastors inform, provide substance, and differentiate their presence from that of other helpers when serving people in the crises of life.

This collection clearly does not provide a comprehensive analysis of the relation of pastoral ministry to theology. It does, however, identify and discuss vital links between two worlds that often are mistakenly perceived as separate and autonomous. As such, the contributors demonstrate the organic and interdependent relation of these two spheres of activity, showing in the process how each would be impoverished if concern for the other were absent. A clarification of the roles and activities of pastors and theologians that are considered necessary for each generation of Christians is undertaken by these authors. It is a task in which they are participating and to which all other concerned Christians are invited.

CHAPTER 1

The Pastor as Theologian

Albert C. Outler

MY TOPIC SEEMS STRAIGHTFORWARD AND CLEAR. IT
focuses on a pair of familiar terms and suggests a set of
interdependent relationships between their distinctive
functions. It presumes a general understanding of what
"pastors" are and what a "theologian" is. Its special problematic concerns the positive "uses," if any, of "theology" to
pastors in their rounds.

But this, of course, is where a variety of ambiguities
begin to turn up. For starters, it is obvious that pastor and
theologian are polysemous terms, with widely different
meanings to different people. For some, the word pastor
has a load of ecclesiastical connotations—betokening the
authorized leader of a particular congregation or parish in
its worship of God and its mission in the world. For others,
the focus is on a pastor's professional status (alongside other
professionals: physicians, lawyers, bankers, undertakers)—

Albert C. Outler, Ph.D., is Emeritus Professor of Theology at Perkins
School of Theology, Southern Methodist University, Dallas.

11

men and women with special training and skills, institutional credentials, and perquisites that go with the territory. In some ears the terms pastor and chaplain sound like synonyms. And some older people recall when pastors were spoken of as parsons—people of eminence in a given place because of their superiority in learning and their acknowledged roles as leaders in the community.

In like fashion, the term theologian generates a variety of notions (not all of them positive). There are those who think of theologians as people who are addicted to high-level abstractions and to the tasks of systematic conceptualizations of religious doctrines. Others think of theologians as professional rationalizers for emotive, often trendy views of religion and culture. Some theologians know a great deal about Christian intellectual history; some seem preoccupied with current issues (or issues that recently have been current). I have a friend who speaks of theologians as "humorless souls overloaded with eager answers to questions rarely asked." These pejorative images carry over to some pastors and prompt them to disavow any suspicion on that point: "I'm not a theologian" (they will say) "but . . ." (after which they will trot out what is actually a theological opinion of one sort or another, usually threadbare). And yet there are pastors (some youngish, and successful!) who speak of themselves as theologians, without discernible embarrassment or immodesty. "I was ordained," said one of them to me recently, "to teach my people about God and the mysteries of faith, and that makes me a theologian. It is one of the functions of my pastoral office."

The problem here is rooted in the distinction in many minds between the pastor's task as practical and people-oriented, and the theologian's task as chiefly theoretical and idea-oriented. Many of us were brought up to think of theology as "systematic" by defintion and in principle. This

12

collides with the fact that there is no *systematic* theology in the Bible, and precious little in the history of Christian thought, until one discovers Peter Lombard (c. 1100–1160) and the Fourth Lateran Council (1215). Since then, however (in the West, at least), the theologian's ideal has been dominated by the vision of a "system of doctrine" that will be orderly, complete, and true. The theological task, therefore, has tended to begin with the problem of method, and to proceed thence to questions of authority and epistemology. How do we know what is real, and how does one "prove" any given assertion or set of assertions? Armed with the proper method and authority, one can tackle the theological topics themselves, *systematically:* God, Jesus Christ, Holy Spirit, Trinity, anthropology, soteriology, ethics, ecclesiology, eschatology.

Given such an ideal image, not many working pastors would set themselves up as theologians. Here is the basis of an oft-assumed conflict of interest between pastors and theologians. There is that old wheeze about the Scottish pastor who fancied himself as a "theologian" and whose sermons were conceived as theological lectures: "He was incomprehensible on Sunday and invisible the rest of the week." Over against this is the image of a pastor as exempt from profound and sustained reflection on the mysteries of God. A recent article in *The Christian Century* commended a certain pastor, whose sermons "might have seemed thin to a theologian, but he was a people-intensive person and he carefully played to his strengths."

It would be absurd to pretend that I am able to sort out all these ambiguities. However, a step toward clarity can be taken by thinking of the term pastor in its traditional sense as the authorized *caretaker* of a designated "flock," or constituency. Most church members are familiar with the notion of a pastor as the representative of a given church, in one of its local congregations (by contrast with the self-elected freelancers, whose "parish" is "the whole world"). Local pastors have a host of things to do, but one of their first duties (in the pulpit and out of it) is to think and speak carefully about God and the Christian gospel, in ways that are faithful to scripture and to Christian experience (both in past ages and the present), that are reasoned and reasonable, *and* that convey a vivid sense of grace and mystery, to those with ears to hear. But such a way of speaking of God in the human venture is at least one of the valid meanings of "theo-logy." Thus conscientious caretakers who can do this well are also theologians. But more, theology in this sense becomes an essential resource for a good pastor.

The word pastor is a faded metaphor; it comes from a culture that, for most of us, is long since unremembered. Time was, though, when there were pastoral societies, and their pastors (i.e., the shepherds) were the linchpins of the pastoral community. In such a culture, relationships between "shepherds" and "sheep" were crucial, and rich with nuances. One of these had to do with the differences between a pastor who had a stake in the community treasure and a "hireling," who chiefly worked for wages. The word for hireling in Greek *(misthotos)* had this connotation (as in John 10:12–13); its Latin equivalent *(mercenarius)* gave us "mercenary" with its clutch of overtones connoting self-interest. The shepherd's prime motivation is care for the sheep; the hirelings are concerned with their own welfare.

The root meaning of pastor (and its cognates), then, is that of the devoted *caretaker,* whose unselfish devotion could be taken for granted. I recall a striking analysis of authority in African societies by Dr. Mercy Oduyoye, of Nigeria, currently a chief executive with the World Council of Churches. Her special emphasis was the notion of a chief as "one whose first business is to look after the others." This accords with that striking definition of greatness as preeminent service that Jesus gave his disciples, and that is remembered in all three synoptic Gospels (Matthew 20:25–28, Mark 10:42–44, Luke 22:26–27). Here is the essence of the pastoral office: one's self-chosen commitment to caretaking ("not to be served but to serve"), and to do whatever this requires in any given set of needs and opportunities.

In pastoral societies the good pastor was a paragon of virtue, and Jesus seems to have understood his own mission in light of this image. It is certain that the early Christians claimed it for him. One of their earliest icons was of Jesus as *pastor bona* ("good shepherd"), holding a lamb on his shoulders. In times of persecution Christian pastors were, in the nature of things, more visible to the mobs and magistrates and, therefore, more vulnerable. It was this "noble army of the martyrs" that greatly impressed the pagans: the manifestation of Christian fortitude in caretaking, even unto death.

When, however, Christianity was first emancipated (by Constantine), and thereafter established as the state religion (by Theodosius I), the pastor's image changed—and not always for the better. Most of the Christian leaders continued to serve faithfully, but the excitements of controversy distracted many, and favors from civil authorities seduced others. Cultivated pagans, like Ammianus Marcellinus, felt aggrieved by the easy acceptance of clerical privileges by Christian bishops (such as free passage on the imperial transport system!).

In medieval times the parish priest found his pastoral dignity secured by the "power of the keys"; it was his exclusive right to absolve repentant sinners and to administer the sacraments of the church to the people. He could, in Gerard Manley Hopkins' vivid phrase, "unhouse and house the Lord."[1] This is still a Roman Catholic priest's unique right and dignity.

Protestantism's rejection of all earthly mediators ("our only Mediator and Advocate, Jesus Christ"[2]) left Protestants' human search for a gracious God focused on "faith alone" *(sola fide)* and on "scripture alone" *(sola Scriptura).* It is easy to see how radically this altered the focus of pastoral caretaking from the sacerdotal mediation of grace to the pastoral interpretation of grace. The pastor thus became a biblical exegete above all else, and a teacher of sound doctrine (as over against those "false doctrines" that were spawned so readily by misguided interpretations of scripture). In addition to the discarded errors of the papacy, there were new distortions in ethics (e.g., antinomianism), new rationalisms, new sectarian controversies, in a society turning secular and desacralized. Leadership in the mainstream Protestant tradition passed from the bishops to a new breed of "professors" (once a term for all professing Christians!). Pastors now responsible for the caretaking of souls who stood accountable to God alone needed the expertise of scholars who understood, better than they, what controvertible texts in the scriptures really meant. New "confessions of faith" became convenient (and authoritative) summaries of "pure doctrine"; most of them were formulated by "professors."

Still, the interpersonal qualities of pastoral caretaking continued to be important. In the different traditions of the so-called magisterial Reformation (Lutheran, Reformed, Anglican) the pastor's *teaching* function continued to be paramount—and this meant academic training, especially in the biblical languages and in Latin, as the shared medium of classical and European culture.

Five centuries later we have lived to see the passing of the parson and the emergence of new patterns of leadership in contemporary churches and in their environing societies. This has involved a lowered status for the clergy partly because of the leveling up of the education of the general public (despite all laments to the contrary!) and the leveling *down* of the educational standards of the clergy, comparatively speaking. Mainstream Protestant denominations have embraced current patterns of business management and current notions of the political process. This has been paralleled by a certain "inflation by degrees," in which the clergy get less basic education and fancier titles for it. A consequence of these complex developments has been decreased prestige for the ordinary pastor and increased attraction of "specializations." An indirect consequence has been a set of temptations for undervalued caretakers to become more careful of their own self-interests!

We know, of course, the age-old tradition of anti-clericalism (from Celsus in the second century to Umberto Eco in our time—not to mention such things as that comic strip *Kudzu*, with its jibes at "spiritual aerobics" and its sardonic slogan for the Rev. Will B. Dunn: "There's no business like soul business"). One thing such criticisms mean for us nowadays, in the desacralized and narcissist society we live in, is a reconsideration, in depth, of the raisons d'être of the pastoral office, in the classical understandings of conscientious caretaking that I have reviewed. What is the special need for a secularized pastor in a society in which Joyce Brothers already knows *How to Get Whatever You Want Out of Life* and in which Nathaniel Branden can teach anyone who will buy his books, *The Psychology of Self Esteem*? In such a culture the pastor as preacher is tempted to turn toward "the human potential" movements as more relevant (and more efficacious) than biblical theology. How should such pastors as counselors be dis-

17

tinguished from all those other beshingled psychologists? Why should a contemporary pastor, with so many administrative responsibilities, look beyond the managerial patterns of well-run corporations? Ludwig Feuerbach argued, a century and a half ago, that "the essence of Christianity" is our love of an idealized "humanity"—a commonplace notion by now, lately reiterated from an unexpected quarter, a Jesuit professor![3] In a culture dominated by Enlightenment visions of human autonomy, progress, and perfectibility, the pastor's role, both as caretaker and as theologian, has been changed yet again, from priest or exegete to counselor and guide to people who are working out their salvation on their own, as visionaries to people who are intent on setting up "the Heavenly City" here on earth—forthwith.[4]

But what if this eighteenth-century vision of Enlightenment and human utopia is fading in the eyes of many thoughtful people in all parts of the earth?[5] What if our old faith in progress and perfectibility is becoming less and less credible? What if we have already entered a post-Enlightenment, postmodern, postliberal epoch in which the tragic dimensions of human existence are increasingly more evident, and when questions like salvation from beyond (salvation by grace) are having to be faced in new contexts, by theologians and secular gurus alike. If something like this is going on, it is at least arguable—and is being argued by a wide array of astute observers of the human condition (artists, intellectuals, diplomats)—that a massive tectonic shift of intellectual climates is taking place, a shift of such magnitude that the human future cannot be foreseen as a further extrapolation of the past millennium. Some are old enough to remember how cocky and confident those bright and cheerful iconoclasts of the 1960s were, who so eagerly volunteered to serve as pallbearers for God's "funeral."

Recently I reviewed the subsequent curricula vitae of the "death of God" theologians, and it was the irony of their recent histories that struck me most forcibly. Not a single one of them has gone on to the harvest of the brave beginnings.

The sum of this litany (and it would take a book to expound it and to update its global geopolitical relevance, what with Muslim fundamentalism on the march, with Christian theology in a new confusion, etc. etc.) is that the office and role of the pastor in a postliberal age must also be included in the list of basic reconsiderations. It will no longer be enough for pastors to be caretakers by appointment, or at their convenience. They will have to find new "identities" in their vocations to replace the outmoded imitations we have had: of pastors as amateur psychiatrists, of pastors as professors in some open university, of pastors as politicians with pulpits for podiums.

For it is clear that in whatever new age may be emerging, the hungers of the human spirit will continue unsatisfied by the empty calories of fake autonomy. The world is awash with unhappiness, among the predators as well as their prey. The powerful suffer from their neuroses (and worse) while the powerless are deprived of their human dignity and worth. For all the progress we have registered in our *rhetoric* of social justice, the substance of basic social reform remains disgracefully insufficient. The inhumane realities of racism, sexism, and uncaring in general persist in a society that *professes* a passion for humane values. Men and women take consolation in crying for "peace, peace," when there is no peace.

But even in such a webwork of illusion the primal landmarks of the Sacred are evident in human experience, when looked for and discerned by seeing eyes. Human beings are still oriented toward their origins and ends, in the divine initiative and purpose still conserved for us in the biblical narrative. That story is still our story: of God's intent in creation and God's patience with its waywardness, the self-defeating strategies of human creatures, with their compulsions to supplant God with idols of their own making. There is still the gospel of the mysterious compassions of divine mercy coming to a bright focus in a humble birth, an incomparable life, a horrid death, and a deathless triumph of faith and hope. And with all these memories and aspirations, however overlaid with alienations, the human need for spiritual caretaking continues. Men and women "of all sorts and conditions" still need words and witness to the Sacred Presence as the "native" climate of the human heart for a sense of at-homeness with the Holy in their midst. Humans still grope for *meaning:* in their homes, in their work, in their unemployment, in hospitals, in precinct meetings, in the shadow of a cross, in the glory of a Shekinah. And this calls for a pastoral wisdom that can act and speak credibly of meanings that surpass experience, even if with a stammering tongue and fallible action. Human beings deserve to understand their existence as *from* God, human life lived *before* God, life upheld *by* God's encompassing presence and omnipotent grace. "Meaning" comes from a deep awareness that life is finite but not happenstance, that all its goods are gifts, that, come weal or woe, God is for us, and that nothing but unbelief can separate us from the love of God which is in Christ Jesus.

For there are men and women of all sorts and conditions, in all ages and cultures whose lives have been nourished by their realization that nothing much comes from the urge to go it alone; and yet that life abundant comes from an upholding Providence that wills love, righteousness, joy, and peace. Such people are undergirded by their confidence in a human future (not just for themselves alone, either) that is safeguarded more by their "participation" in God's sovereign grace than by any other human achievement. Some such faith as this is nurtured by men and women who share and show it, and who devote their lives to "looking after others" out of their commitments to "the Rule of *God* and of *God's* righteousness." It is caretaking in this spirit that would satisfy Jesus' mandate to the good pastor: *"Feed* my sheep."

Rhetoric like this may sound distressingly quaint to men and women who have grown up under the recent embargo against "God-talk." It will also seem distressingly unscientific to those whose horizons have not been stretched beyond the "empirical." To such people, pastors must seem either redundant or as bit players in the secular scene. However, in that scene, pastors are at a grave disadvantage, no matter how earnest. Few of them understand the bafflement of economics (but then who else does?). In the splendid enterprises of modern medicine some pastors have earned their places on "the healing team," but only as auxiliaries. As politicians, the track record of pastors is depressing, whether as bigots on the right or passionaries on the left. Nowadays few pastors become outstanding civic leaders, but remain as inviting targets for gossip and scandal. And the pastor who lives by his or her "public relations" is pathetically dependent on the fickle winds of "publicity."

This is not to say that the good pastor ought not to be concerned to be a fully involved citizen, or an effective therapist within appropriate limits, or a scholar, or whatever else serves society. God be praised for all pastors who are cultivated and creative, but let us pray to be saved from editorials dressed up as sermons. We should be grateful for all zeal with knowledge, all social activism that is nonpar-

21

tisan and nonviolent. But the good pastor must have a prime concern for human values, defined by God. In terms like these the pastor can think, feel, and speak as few others can, with an authority derived from a community of faith. It is, therefore, part of the good pastor's functions: this careful, prayerful, sense-making talk about God, and the import of God's reality and grace for a truly and fully human existence. But "sense-making talk about God" is also what is meant by the term *theo-logia,* and thus helps to identify the pastor as a "theo-logian." We know this from familiar lexical parallels: a *geo*-logist (from the Greek word for earth, *gē*), a *bio*-logist (*bios* is Greek for life), a *psycho*-logist (where *psyche* is Greek for whatever it is that constitutes the prime topic of psychology).

A good pastor has a right and duty to be able to speak of many things, with the proviso that the talk be informed, articulate, and relevant. A good pastor also has a duty to *listen,* carefully, to what other people say, to discern what they *mean* by what they say and how they say it, and what they mean by what they leave unsaid. But beyond this it is the pastor's special ordination to speak of *God,* knowledgeably enough so as to awaken and inform the inborn sense of the Sacred and to interpret its import for living. This is the essence of the theo-logian's venture. The pastor as theologian is one who is familiar with accrued and collective wisdom of the Christian community through the centuries (in its multiform traditions). The pastor is competent in the critical use of discursive reason (and firm to resist nonsense even when disguised as piety). And the end of all this is not a bare assent of the mind, but a personal *experience* of God's reconciling love.

But even this view of *theo-logia* needs probing and pondering. The word itself seems to have been coined by Aristotle to denote our presumed knowledge of transcendent reality. Afterward it was borrowed by Varro and Cicero for their comments on the involvements of the gods in human affairs (*De natura deorum;* note their *plurals*). No such term appears in the Bible, despite the fact that the central reality within its narrative, first and last, is the self-communication of the One God and this God's involvement in creation and history. The Hebrews preferred circumlocutions about the Divine Name. Despite all their various "titles" for deity, they have no definitions (unless you count that oracle in Exodus 3:14 about "I AM THAT I AM"). The New Testament people were more explicit in their "God-talk," but always in terms that are apophantic and metaphorical.[6] Both testaments are frankly anthropomorphic, and never anthropocentric (which is why both sexist *and* antisexist literalism is as bad as any other literalism; it is wiser and more truly monotheistic to hold with the classic designation of God as "everlasting, without body, parts or passions, of infinite power, wisdom and goodness"). The scriptures are full of God-talk *(theo-logia);* they are laden with "signs" of God's concerns for human creation. But they are clear on the point that no human "knowledge of God" gives us any control over God (save for our God-granted power of a sort of veto that is, tragically, self-stultifying!). Biblical *theo-logia* is coherent and unitary, but it is nowhere systematized, that is, reduced to topics arranged in some logical order, with all the major options laid out argumentatively. Methodically speaking, one could say that biblical *theo-logia* is typically ad hoc and functional. This fact has disconcerted many moderns, who have tried valiantly to remedy such a deficiency (as in Gerard Von Rad's *Old Testament Theology* and Rudolf Bultmann's *Theology of the New Testament*). It may or may not strike *post*modern minds as odd that each of these systematizations turns out to have been, in significant measure, a mirror image to the systematizer's own theology!

In the patristic and Middle Ages the term *theo-logia* was used rather sparsely and variously, usually to refer to *theologoumena* (plausible opinions) or as in summaries (e.g., John of Damascus, *De Fide Orthodoxa*). In the mid-twelfth century a tidy-minded man, Peter Lombard, undertook to remedy the spreading discord by collecting representative opinions on all the fundamental theological topics in a systematic treatise entitled *The Sentences* (i.e., summations of doctrinal teachings) *in Four Books*. This methodological innovation attracted the attention of theologians for at least two centuries, and set a trend that has persisted down to our times. Having served his apprenticeship in commenting on Lombard's *Sentences*, Thomas Aquinas produced two magnificent summations of his own, one for non-Christians and the other for Christians who needed their doctrinal confusions sorted out. In his preface to the *Summa Theologiae* he comments on the virtual impossibility of any such task (and he did not live to finish it; but then neither did Karl Barth in his similar venture seven centuries later). Aquinas dutifully warns his students not to impede Christian understanding "by the swarm of irrelevant questions, articles and arguments."[7]

What is most relevant for us about the "Angelic Doctor's" achievement, however, is less its awesome architectonic than the atmosphere in which he thought and wrote. The times were in turmoil; the tone of the *Summae* is quiet and calm, and prayerful. This is theology *coram Deo* (talking about God as in God's living presence). But this means that one need not be a genius in order to cultivate his mood, and his remembrance, for example, that Augustine's *Confessions* had been an extended (and sometimes intricate) prayer.

With the tragic rupture in the heart and mind of Western Christianity in the sixteenth century, *theo-logia* took on a more combative tone and temper. Modern theology (Protestant *and* Roman Catholic) was conceived in bitterness, baptized in blood and bile, nurtured in controversy. Its gladiatorial fury repelled gentler souls like Philipp Melanchthon among the Protestants and Luis Molina among the Romans. On the other side, however, it excited many a mean spirit (e.g., Flaccius, Gomarus, Torquemada).

For two centuries, a great wealth of intellectual talent and zeal was devoted without stint to a clamorous search for *the* true theological system. The eventual failure of this scholasticism left a complex prejudice that is still powerful: theology is technical; theology is polemic; theology is rarely edifying to "plain people." Worse yet, a contrary prejudice was generated. Good pastors, concerned above all for the spiritual caretaking of their people, were encouraged to leave the tasks of speculative theology to others, and to concentrate on their more "practical" duties. This, however, had the unfortunate effect of canceling Anselm's time-honored formula for pastoral theology: *fides quaerens intellectum* (faith in search of credibility). In turn, this allowed the pietists to sanctify their anti-intellectualism.

Friedrich Schleiermacher, half pietist, half "man of the Enlightenment," sought to set the balances right with his threefold reconception of "theology," aimed at preparing pastors with orientations for their encounters with half-convinced Christians, on the one hand, and cultured non-believers, on the other. His first point was that true religion is not a "knowing," but a "living." Second, Christian faith revives in the hardened human heart the experience of God's just judgment of sin *and* of God's unmerited pardoning love. Third, religion is sustained by the honest recognition of our radical dependence on the grace of just such a God.

It is a personal embarrassment to leave so sketchy a historical overview. This, however, may be just as well, for the history of theology has, for most people, seemed so largely dominated by the theological titans. Now, for the time being at least, the age of the titans is over. Thus pastors with more nearly normal talents have to come to terms with the fact that the business of theology is far too important to be left to the current professionals. It is more fruitful to notice that Ephesians 4:11 links the roles of pastors *and* teachers, and that it is the Holy Spirit who endues this double office with special gifts. Pastors are, preeminently, teachers; and teachers are, preeminently, guides and midwives to insight and inquiry. The good pastor is also a good teacher. On the human scale he or she is a sort of "paraclete," to lead inquiring minds into the mystery and truth of God and God's dealings with the human family, over the long stretches of human time and in the exigencies of contemporary experience. Such teachers are not often theologians' theologians, and need not be. Rather, they are *folk*-theologians whose special gift and privilege is to bestir the sense of the Sacred in ordinary mortals, to guide plain people into a living faith in the Holy God. And all such teaching and guiding is theo-logical insofar as it is concerned with God, as God, and insofar as it leads sensitive souls to live and think and enjoy and suffer, and die, *in God's gracious and upholding presence*.

The ordinary pastor as theologian need not be eligible for membership in the American Theological Society. He or she would, however, have to understand and recognize the theological issues that are always embedded in religious affairs of every kind, so as to be able to link any current commotion with its biblical analogues and illuminations, and to safeguard theological notions from "ho-hum-ness," on the one side, and "oh-wow-ness," on the other. The pastor as theologian need not be eloquent (though that always helps), but must have a love of the language and a lively sense of its mysterious power to convey meanings that reach farther into the Sacred Mystery than flat prose ever can, or even poetry.

Pastors as theologians will understand the problematic quality of all claimed knowledge of transcendent being. Thus they will be able to deal honestly and fairly with skeptics and with their faith in the *non*existence of God. They will recognize the biblical priorities, of the love of God before all else and the love of all else, *in God*. This will then make more sense out of the imperative to "seek first the kingdom of God and *God's* righteousness," as the first premise of a theocentric ethic. They will have seen through the fatuous delusions in our current narcissisms (as reflected in those portentous television ads that assure the self-indulgent: "You can have it all" and "Your world should know no boundaries"). But, as caretakers of "lost" sheep, they will live in genuine compassion with the tragedies of so much unlived life, so much half-lived life, and so much stifled life as there is in the world. This, in turn, will fuel an involvement (that must be more competent than merely emotive) in all God's good causes in the world, most of which call on the caretaker for quiet self-oblation. And all this must be woven into the dynamisms of those needful routines of parish life, with its ingatherings of faith-seeking folk into the *koinonia* of Christ, and its constructive outreach into the community.

So much, then, for a pastor's chief function as a theologian—speaking thoughtfully and convincingly about God, as if in God's Presence and by the power of God's Spirit. But such speech (however profound or clear) is never a fruitful end in itself. Theology reaches out beyond itself, from speaking about God to confident and direct address to God. Prayer, praise, and communion have the power to turn thoughtful and critical reflection into a reverent "walking in the Spirit" (see Gal. 5:25).

Pastors as theologians will understand that although abstractions cannot substitute for prayer, they can enrich its substance; that although prayer cannot substitute for action, it can energize and guide it. Jesus' first disciples recognized their need for such an enrichment and guidance, and besought their newfound "pastor" to teach them to pray: to speak to God as well as about God. The "sample prayer" he gave them still serves to disclose the nature of prayer itself and to manifest its inner spirit. It stands squarely in the tradition of an ancient call to prayer that every devout Jew knows well as primal, the great *Shema* of Deuteronomy 6:4–5.

The textual history of the Lord's Prayer in the Gospel according to Matthew is a curious one, and illumines a crucial nuance in a pastor's theological understanding: the difference between dialogue and doxology. In our oldest manuscripts the Prayer concludes with the petition for deliverance from evil. This ending was retained in the Roman Mass, where it was followed by a prayer (in preparation for communion) that repeats the last petition: "Deliver us, we beseech thee, O Lord, from all evils: past, present and yet to come." But a similar doxology appears in the *Didache*, obviously borrowed from 1 Chronicles 29:11–13, and this same combination appears in the Liturgy of St. John Chrysostom. Indeed, in later manuscripts of Matthew's Gospel, the Prayer and the doxology stand together. In the Reformation this was preferred by Wycliffe, and Luther after him.

It is less helpful to emphasize these variations, as if they were a problem, than to probe their deeper import. The Prayer bespeaks an entire commitment: the offertory of both life and self-interest into God's good care and keeping ("*thy* Name," "*thy* Kingdom," "*thy* Will"). The doxology is a climactic affirmation that all such commitments are secured for us by God's sovereign grace and providence. But note that prayers are always at risk of being pattered (a word to remind us of what happens to "Paternosters" when they are merely rattled off). Thus, just as it is the pastor-theologian's duty to warn off the faithful from mindless God-talk, it is urgent that they be saved from "vain repetitions." The sign of both these jobs well done is when pastor and people are moved to prayer together, with one heart and voice—and to add a grateful and confident doxology, in every case: "For *thine* is the kingdom, and the power, and the glory, for ever. Amen."

CHAPTER 2

Black Theology and Pastoral Ministry
A Challenge to Ecumenical Renewal and Solidarity

Gayraud S. Wilmore

THE QUESTION IS FREQUENTLY ASKED, WHY DID IT SEEM important for African American Christians to develop a black theology at the very time that Martin Luther King Jr. was leading all Americans—black and white, Protestants, Catholics, and Jews—toward a theological position and an ethics that renounced and sought to abolish all discrimination on the basis of racial and ethnic differences?

Another closely related question is sometimes phrased, Is it not true that black theology is essentially a political strategy? What possible relevance can it have to the normal ministry of the church, to the responsibility of pastors to lead their people into the kind of psychological health and spiritual maturity that will help them to deal with the daily problems of life and death through a saving faith in Jesus

Gayraud S. Wilmore, S.T.M., is Dean and Professor of Afro-American Religious Studies at New York Theological Seminary in New York City.

Christ? Does not this theology seem alien to pastoral ministry?

A third question, particularly critical for ecumenical renewal and solidarity between white and black Christians, may be put in this way: What can a theology designated by reference to skin color, ethnicity, or culture have to do with what might be called "basic *Christian* theology"? Is it not true that black theology is so focused on the black experience as to lose any real significance for Christians who are not of African descent or members of black churches?

These are challenging questions, indeed! No simplistic, or even definitive answers should be expected to negotiate all the difficult problems of ontology, epistemology, sociology, value theory, and ethics (to mention only some of the disciplines involved) that resist any superficial analysis or casual interest. Having registered this demurrer, however, let me hasten to add that such questions as these must be honestly faced by the black theologian. But it is equally certain that white theologians must be prepared for difficult answers that will challenge their most serious and thoughtful consideration.

All theologies are human ways of thinking and talking about God out of a particular context. All theologies are qualified by time, geography, culture, and the material conditions of existence. It is not possible to understand the religious commitments and theologies of a people, or to bond with them ecumenically, without approaching their thought-life with humility, sensitivity, and an openness to differences from one's own position. The time is past when white theologians and ethicists can expect to understand black theology, or to contribute to ecumenical unity and renewal, without knowing the history, studying the texts, and seeking to appropriate for themselves the subtlety and complexity of the black religious experience in the United States.

Nor can white theologians any longer assume that all God-talk must be in the form of the abstract, literary language characteristic of theological discourse contingent on philosophical modalities derived from ancient Greek and Roman civilizations. This Eurocentric mode of thinking and talking about God is only one model. We African Americans are, after all, an oral people. We prefer to paint pictures with words that convey our feelings, moods, and motivations rather than with words that convey abstract ideas and concepts. We prefer to sing our philosophies, to tell our stories, and to write poetry that expresses our ideas better than systematic theologies in the Western tradition. In this discussion of the thought-world and pastoral implications of black theology it seems most appropriate to create a mood, a context, a universe of intimate discourse within which experimental and tentative answers to my three initial questions may be explored. What I say in the following pages, therefore, will not so much solve all the questions raised by black theology as to point in the direction of answers or solutions still largely inarticulate or imperfectly construed in the discursive, analytical language of systematic theology. This is one reason some black theologians have elected to speak of black theology as a "pastoral theology," but with broader implications that have to do with our continuing struggle for liberation.

I will address the three questions raised above consecutively. In the course of attempting to answer them I will explore black theology as a particular way of doing Christian theology in the United States, how it came to be what it is today out of both a relatively distant and more recent history, and—most important for this essay—the function it serves in pastoral ministry within the black church. Finally, as suggested by the third question, I will argue that appreciation and understanding, on the part of white Christians, of this form of doing theology out of the pastor's study and also the streets, out of prayer and political action, can help to close the widening gap between black and white churches in the United States and enhance the whole ecumenical movement, particularly as it impinges on relations between the developed and the developing worlds.

Theology and the Color Line

W.E.B. DuBois made the famous statement that the problem of the twentieth century is the problem of the color line.[1] What did he mean? He was making the point that race and color have ontological significance in white Western societies. He was saying that the mystique of race, symbolized in the United States by blackness and whiteness, would present an inescapable problem to our thinking, our feeling, our politics and economics, our religion and culture for at least a hundred years. If DuBois was right—and I believe he was—it makes little sense to talk in the West about a Christian theology that is somehow unaffected by the problem of race and ethnicity. The race problem is ubiquitous in the United States. We breathe it in the air. We take it in with our mothers' milk.

In February 1987, at an international conference on negritude and Afro cultures in the Americas, I heard a black Peruvian anthropologist, Dr. Victoria Santa Cruz, say that when she was a young girl, black mothers told their children that there was a stream between earth and heaven that everyone had to cross over when they died. When blacks who were going to heaven crossed that stream their ugly black color would disappear and they would all turn

33

white. "Often as a young girl," she said, "I wanted to die so I could find that passage and become white!"

Such a story does not shock me. When I was a young boy growing up in the streets of north Philadelphia, there was a saying that circulated among us boys. A folk aphorism that had evidently been passed down from generation to generation it went like this:

> Dark man born of a dark woman, sees dark days.
> He rises up in the morning like a hopper-grass,
> He is cut down in the evening like aspara-grass.

Where did such a saying come from? That is one of the mysteries of African American folklore. No one knows. But notice in this little maxim of the streets a faint allusion to Psalm 90:5–6 (KJV): "They are like grass which groweth up. In the morning it flourisheth, and groweth up; in the evening it is cut down, and withereth."

It is, obviously, a very biblical saying and suggests how a folk theology evolves among a common people who are steeped in the language of scripture. But to find these bitter words pertaining to skin color on the lips of young children also tells a sad story about the consciousness of color among Philadelphia youth in my boyhood, and how it helped to shape our self-identity in the ghetto of the City of Brotherly Love.

But there were other proverbs and adages, like "The blacker the berry, the sweeter the juice." Moreover, for almost two hundred years the black church celebrated the blackness of Ebed-melech, who rescued Jeremiah; the Ethiopian eunuch who was baptized by Philip, the evangelist; Simon of Cyrene, who carried our Lord's cross up the heights of Calvary; and other biblical figures and texts that show that God did not despise God's black children, as some white Christians believed, but through suffering and

34

struggle prepared them for a great destiny. Countless sermons have been preached in black churches on that theme in Psalm 68:31 (KJV): "Princes shall come out of Egypt; Ethiopia shall soon stretch out her hands unto God." Such was the raw material of a black theology of liberation for more than two hundred years.

So it should come as no surprise that for millions of black believers, African American ethnicity is inseparable from the doing of theology, and the theology that evolves from reflection on that ethnicity, in the light of the gospel and in the context of the racism of Western civilization, is not some *other* theology that stands over against a genuine Christian theology that is the property of the white church. Black theology *is* Christian theology without qualification. Jesus Christ authenticates our will to be—to survive as black people in a white racist environment. Jesus Christ must have to do with our affirmation of black being and power, or he was not involved in our creation, does not know who we are, and therefore cannot be our Savior.

When young black people accuse Christianity of being a "white man's religion," they are saying that they have not been taught the rudiments of what we now call black theology. They are expressing distress at the failure of the black church to portray Jesus Christ as the black Messiah who not only satisfies their yearning for affirmation as negated human beings, but also takes on himself their blackness in a world dominated by whites.

Dr. King began to appreciate the agony of our young people toward the end of his life, and although he did not outwardly affirm black theology as such, one sees in sermons and writings in the period just preceding his assassination a turn toward blackness as providential and destined for a special role in the economy of God. In his last book he spoke of black people being called "to imbue

35

our nation with the ideals of a higher and nobler order."
Many black theologians before him had made a similar
messianic claim for black faith. He was speaking out of a
tradition that began as early as the eighteenth century.

> This is our challenge. If we will dare to meet it honestly,
> historians in future years will have to say there lived a great
> people—a black people—who bore their burdens of op-
> pression in the heat of many days and who, through tenac-
> ity and creative commitment, injected a new meaning into
> the veins of American life.[2]

This sense of what I have elsewhere referred to as a
"comprehensive cultural vocation"[3] and the reconstruction
of the theology of the black church that it implies have
imposed an enormous burden on sensitive black pastors,
church executives, and academics. For many pastors it
meant, first of all, finding a way to respond to the challenges of the Black Power movement in which God seemed
to be awakening the black church and community to realities about America that both had sought vainly to evade.

During the 1960s, all over the nation but particularly in
such cities as New York, Philadelphia, Detroit, Cleveland,
Chicago, Los Angeles, and the San Francisco Bay area,
where young freedom fighters of the civil rights struggle
were concentrated, black preachers were faced with a for-
midable competitor for "the souls of black folk." This was
not the first time they had been challenged by rebellious
forces in the ghetto that vied with the church for definitive
interpretation of the signs of the times. That had happened
in the early decades of this century when fraternal organizations, social clubs, business groups, trade unions, the
National Association for the Advancement of Colored People, and the National Urban League had all, each in its own
way, helped to unseat the black minister from the center of

community power and decision-making. The difference was that most of those groups were either spawned by the churches or loosely affiliated with them. They shared, in a general way, the same philosophy of peaceful progress and racial integration that the churches espoused.

The new urban organizations of the mid-1960s were different. The small, disciplined cadres that were involved in (though by no means to be held responsible for) the northern city rebellions were neither in tune with the southern movement led by Martin Luther King Jr., nor with the official leadership of the national black denominations. Perhaps the most we can now say about the ideological stance of those new grassroots organizations is that they were aggressively black nationalist in terms of domestic policy, Pan-Africanist, and oriented toward Fidelism and the Latin American revolution in terms of international affairs. Most of the individuals in such groups were sharply critical, by 1965, of King's moderate politics and Christian pacifism, without being rigidly opposed to the courageous movement he was leading in the south. Following the rhetoric of Malcolm X, the Black Power philosophy of Stokely Carmichael and H. Rap Brown, and the cultural nationalism of Mulana Ron Karenga and Amiri Baraka, these young people changed the vocabulary of the northern struggle from what the newspapers reported as "random rioting and looting" to "organized civil rebellion." Not a few black Christians, seminary professors, assorted artists, intellectuals, and grassroots activists were ineluctably drawn into their ranks. I remember how many "respectable" Methodists, Presbyterians, and Episcopalians I found participating in the first national Black Power conference in Newark, New Jersey, where many of the ideas and commitments that were voiced were contrary to everything familiar to us within the sacred precincts of the churches. But

37

perhaps a story will more clearly illustrate the pressures we experienced during those days, and the direction our religious thought was beginning to take.

In the midst of the Brooklyn uprising in the summer of 1964 one black pastor, whom I shall call Reverend Black, came to the reluctant conclusion that dawned, sometimes with the force of a Damascus road experience, on many of his fellow pastors and church leaders who were trying—under the most difficult circumstances—to give faithful and intelligent leadership to their people during that strange, twilight time for black innocence in the United States.[4]

One night my friend Reverend Black learned that some of the young people from his church were under siege in a riot area that the police had cordoned off. He instinctively knew what had to be done. He drove his car to the roadblock and, pretending to be on an errand that had nothing to do with the riot, broke the law by deceiving the police. Once inside, in the midst of the noise and confusion, Reverend Black rounded up his youngsters, threw their gasoline cans and homemade weapons into the trunk, and then drove a carload of young guerrillas to safety by telling the police another lie to prevent them from searching the car. It was, he said later, the strangest night of his life. Most important, it changed his way of doing theology.

Reverend Black and many other young black clergy like him were brought face to face with the fact that some of the people of their congregations and neighborhoods—people to whom they had been preaching about justice and the meaning of the world struggle for liberation from oppression—were out there in the streets with bricks and Molotov cocktails. The people had chosen the white police, who patrolled their neighborhoods like an army of occupation in some foreign colony, as the most immediate symbol of the racist society, which, they were convinced, had to be resisted by any means possible.

On that particular night Reverend Black realized that he could no longer rely on the resources of his seminary education to supply the theological and ethical guidelines for his preaching and teaching in that volatile situation in Bedford-Stuyvesant. Bonhoeffer, Niebuhr, and Bennett, the social Christianity and political liberalism of Union Seminary and *Christianity and Crisis* may have provided a hermeneutic for understanding what King's movement was about, but they were practically useless in this urban ghetto context of the North. As the crisis deepened, Reverend Black realized what white theologians could not supply the answers he and his people needed for the new questions that were rising with increasing intensity—questions about black history, black consciousness, and violent resistance to unrelenting oppression.

Black was one of the first ministers I knew in New York who began to speak of the bankruptcy of white theology and the need for a new black perspective on the gospel of Jesus Christ. He became one of the early leaders of the National Conference of Black Churchmen, organized in 1967, which adopted the first official statement on black theology at its third national convocation in Oakland, California.[5] And so Reverend Black and many other young pastors, together with a few academics and church bureaucrats, began to reflect theologically about the liberation struggle of black people, not before, but literally in the midst of trying to minister to our people who had themselves sensed that a new obedience was demanded. People who had accepted the gospel from our lips and our writings, now insisted on some demonstration of its realism and practicality in the struggle for liberation from racism and poverty in the United States. It was nothing less than a crisis of credibility for the church of Jesus Christ.

So black theology is not something strange and illicit for black thinkers to be involved in as they try to make sense of the Christian faith. Not only did Martin Luther King Jr. not repudiate the implications of black theology and accepted its basic presuppositions toward the end of his life, but black pastors created black theology in the trenches. It can be regarded as partly a *pastoral* theology because it originated among pastors and church leaders who were trying to find a way to minister to their congregations in a time of revolution.

Pastoral Theology in the Context of Struggle

My second question asked what possible relevance can this way of thinking have to pastoral ministry. I shall never forget when James Forman spoke to the General Assembly of the United Presbyterian Church in San Antonio in the spring of 1969. On the night before his speech I found myself engaged in a long, heated discussion with a group of young urban guerrillas whom I had permitted to occupy my hotel suite. Our conversation centered around the idea of reparations and the Bible, the relevance, or irrelevance, of belief in Christ and the black church for liberation. At the climax of the argument, as proof of their determination to carry through a desperate action against the Presbyterian Church—to demonstrate their willingness to be sacrificed for the black revolution—they pulled out from under my bed two wooden boxes tightly packed with automatic weapons and ammunition. I learned later that this ordnance had been shipped by Greyhound bus from Miami, although I cannot say that Jim Forman knew anything about their plans to intimidate the General Assembly, forcing a vote for reparations to Forman's Black Economic Development Conference the next day.

To say that I was shocked with the discovery of those weapons in my room would be the understatement of my life. I had to assume that my young guests were deadly serious. I tried to disguise my anxiety, verging on panic, as we continued to discuss whether such a tactic as violent confrontation could be strategically and ethically justified. The image in my mind as I argued was that of a ludicrous stickup on the stage of the San Antonio convention hall, with the consequences of a bloody confrontation with the police and the Federal Bureau of Investigation that would set the racial justice cause back a hundred years.

We talked all night. The discussion ranged over what it means to be black and Christian in an oppressive, racist society. We ruminated about God's judgment in political and cultural struggle. We dialogued about the apostasy of the church and what kind of theology and praxis would do justice to the legitimate grievances of disillusioned young black people and, at the same time, remain faithful to the demands of the gospel. We discussed the Black Muslims, holy war, and Jesus Christ as the liberator of the outcast and the downtrodden.

When the sun finally came up over San Antonio I emerged from that smoke-polluted hotel room unshaven and bone-weary. I was not really sure what the young people would do that day. But I knew that I had been their pastor that night—perhaps the only pastor most of them had ever known. I knew that what was troubling their souls had an external source in our racist society. I knew that during that long night I as their pastor and they as my young, unintended congregation had in fact been creating a black theology of liberation.

One of those young men was Irving Davis, of Teaneck,

New Jersey, who had been in charge of a sit-in at the Interchurch Center in New York, and later became a close friend with whom I worked in the National Conference of Black Churchmen. Irving also became something of a black lay theologian. When he died on April 22, 1981, as a result of injuries suffered in an "accident" in Tanzania that many of us believe was arranged by the Central Intelligence Agency, I wrote an editorial for *Presbyterian Outlook* entitled "A Prophet Without Portfolio." I wanted other Christians to know that Irving Davis was a member of that "invisible church" to which I and others had ministered as pastors and allies during the 1960s. But here is something interesting about pastoral ministry under the conditions of social struggle: *we become pastors to one another.* The truth was that it was Irving Davis who ministered to public Christians like me and taught some of us in the church how to lay down our lives for the brothers and sisters. And so I wrote in part:

> I will remember Irving Davis most for what he did for me and several other clergy who were drawn, sometimes kicking and screaming, into the magnetic field of his vision of what the churches should be about in Africa and the Caribbean. Some of us used to say that we evangelized this hard-nosed black revolutionary who came to throw a monkey wrench into the ecclesiastical machinery which he believed was grinding the faces of the oppressed, and stayed to become a partner in mission and a brother. We now know that he evangelized us.[6]

The point of all this is not to glorify young black revolutionaries, or to present black theology as a new situation ethics or a form of black antinomianism that justifies anything and calls it Christian as long as it serves the cause of black liberation. I simply want to make two points: First, that many black pastors were forced to face the problem of having to minister to disillusioned and dispirited young people during the 1960s and 1970s, and it was out of the struggle to find meaning and redemption in the cause of black dignity and liberation that a contemporary black theology came into existence. Second, the new black theology that we were developing was partly a *pastoral* theology. Rooted in the experience of the black church, it sought to bring the gospel of Jesus Christ to bear upon the most exasperating problems of marginalized and cynical people—mainly young people—in the frustrated and alienated black community that was becoming more and more restive within the belly of the great white whale of America.

Much better than anything else I could say, the two incidents I have cited illustrate the pastoral dilemma many black clergy found themselves in during the 1960s and early 1970s as we attempted to interpret the events of the time in the light of the gospel and combat the allegation that Christianity was nothing more than "the white man's religion," having nothing to do with black liberation. Whatever can be said about the truth or error of our new theology, it did not emerge from libraries, doctoral dissertations, and quiet lectures in seminary classrooms, but out of physical strain, emotional distress, and intellectual conflict in the streets. But it also issued from a new enthusiasm, a bounding sense of hope, an experience that can best be described to Western Christians by the Greek term *kairos*, a moment of blinding revelation that the times are suddenly full of transcendent meaning and that an ultimate decision must be made whether to be faithful or faithless to the God who is one's creator and redeemer. Such a *kairos*, a moment of unprecedented illumination and urgent decision-making, came many times between 1955 and 1975,

43

and it is perhaps only now—many years later and at a time of sadly diminished commitment to revolutionary struggle in the United States—that we can appreciate what God was doing with us. The theological reflection and social action that were to accompany and flow from those confrontations with what Dr. King called the *Zeitgeist*, the spirit of the age, or "the forces of history and the forces of destiny,"[7] were basically pragmatic and pastoral.

Despite the legitimate ethical questions that arise out of the two stories I have related, it is important to remember that black theology did not present itself as a new situation ethic, an antinomian philosophy that justifies anything deemed necessary for the success of our desperate strategies. Although it is unlikely that most pastors agreed with the burning and recklessness that some groups engaged in, it must be said that many felt the sting of oppression and the urgency of resistance sufficiently to identify with the revolutionaries, to have an "understanding and compassion" for those young people who were, after all, *our* sons and daughters. It was indeed a time for counsel and pastoral guidance to a radical sector of the black community, but what kind of counseling, and to what end?

If we ministers are to be accused of a certain naiveté about ideological corruption and of having too easily identified the cause of the poor and oppressed with God's cause, I for one am prepared to concede it. If anything authenticated Reverend Black's response to his young people and mine to the would-be guerrillas in my hotel suite—whom I might have, on cooler consideration, immediately turned over to the police—it was the profound feeling, which I choose to call the internal testimony of the Holy Spirit, that we were *right*.

Looking back today I can only affirm, with the apostle Paul, that it was "the Spirit himself bearing witness with

our spirit" that we were children, heirs, and fellow suf-
ferers with Christ (see Romans 8:15–17); or so it seemed to
us. Nothing seemed more truly God's will than to take the
side of the black poor in the fight for justice, calling them in
the name of Jesus Christ, who himself was poor and marginalized, to a new vision of the world, a liberated existence
free from the racism and hedonism of a greed-motivated,
selfish, and materialistic culture. Some may call it idealism,
but a pneumatological basis undergirded our conviction
that even if mistakes were made, we were on the right
track. The Holy Spirit in the black church sanctified our
praxis and gave us the assurance that the old wineskins
could no longer bear the new wine we were imbibing.[8]
There was no doubt in our minds that what Dr. King called
"the beloved community" of all people would be the end of
our striving.

Although he did not live long enough to lend his enormous prestige to the new theological movement that burst
upon the nation during the last years of his life, black
theology was a further extension of the militant reorienta-
tion that Dr. King had given to the black church and
community. James H. Cone and the black theologians who
rallied around him after the publication of his *Black Power
and Black Theology* in 1969[9] did not so much change the
direction of the movement as they deepened its theological
analysis, relating it more to black history and culture and
making it more responsive to the growing impatience of the
masses. Because Cone himself was one of the young radi-
cals of the period, he, more than any of us who were
already in the streets with King, understood what the
younger generation was demanding of the church. Cone
had the youthful audacity, the intellectual aptitude, and
the education to criticize our obsequious dependence on
white theology, and to lead us to a new perspective at a

time when blacks were asking their religious leaders for a new and more relevant word "from the Lord"—a word of judgment, courage, and hope.

Survival, Elevation, and Liberation

Anyone who is called to minister to a black urban congregation whose members are conscious of their African American heritage, to appreciate the religious meaning of the struggle out of poverty and powerlessness, and to understand that that struggle continues today not only in South Africa, but in the south Bronx and almost every other urban community in the nation as well, cannot remain indifferent about our dependence on the conventional theology of the white churches. Frankly, most white theologians have been too insensitive to the black experience to have much to teach black folk about God. They have too often assumed that black faith was little more than a poor carbon copy of their own Euro-American version of the real thing.

It is not surprising, therefore, that the black church's grounding in African spirituality, its political salience and sense of comprehensive cultural vocation almost completely escape the attention of most white scholars. The late Bishop Joseph Johnson Jr., of the Christian Methodist Episcopal Church, one of the most articulate interpreters of black theological reflection, observed:

> For more than one hundred years, Black students have studied in predominantly white seminaries, and have been served a theological diet created, mixed, and dosed out by white theological technicians. The Black seminarians took both the theological milk and meat, and even when they consumed these, their souls were still empty. Those of us who attended white seminaries passed our courses in the

four major fields of study; we knew our Barth and Brunner, and we entered deeply into the serious study of Bonhoeffer and Tillich. But now we have discovered that while these white theologians have elucidated a contemporary faith for white men, they know nothing about the Black experience. To many of the white scholars, the Black experience was (and is) illegitimate and inauthentic.[10]

But black theological reflection independent of white scholarship is not new. From the beginning, black theology was Christian theology that had been reinterpreted by black believers in an effort to understand what the gospel had to do with their struggle to survive genocide, to elevate themselves and their families to a higher quality of life and culture, and to free themselves and all people who needed liberation from every form of domination. The evidence from the slave narratives, the spirituals, sermons, addresses, and the reports of missionaries shows that from the eighteenth century, survival, elevation, and liberation were primary concerns of the slave community and the persistent themes of religious thought in the black community.

Black religion helped the slaves and the tiny communities of free blacks to maintain a modicum of mental health and stoic self-preservation in the face of terror and absurdity. It was the power of the Holy Spirit, felt in the ecstasy of worship and in times of personal crisis and adversity, that kept the folk alive and enabled them to hold body and soul together when everything else was falling apart. Religion was part of their strategy of survival. It made it possible for them to resist the resignation and hopelessness that constantly threatened. The emphasis on the Holy Spirit, personal salvation, and sanctified living became the hallmarks of black folk religion. The survival orientation developed during slavery broke through the urban revivals of black Holiness and Pentecostalism in the early twentieth

47

century and remains a powerful factor in black theological reflection.

A second basic concern and major element in black Christianity during the nineteenth century was "elevation," or the moral, educational, and cultural reform and advancement of the race. Particularly in the writings of free blacks and in their organized efforts one finds this accent on racial uplift prominently displayed. During most of the century the church was the center of the community and played a dominant role in the establishment of the value system and standards of family life, social intercourse, religious and secular education, recreation, and almost every activity that had to do with the edification and refinement of a crude and illiterate people. The church not only provided a meeting place for most of the causes of the community, but also was frequently the initial patron or sponsor of musical, literary, and other cultural endeavors designed to bring beauty and meaning into lives that would otherwise have been drab and meaningless.

The idea of the black church's cultural vocation, a divine calling to be God's agency for ordering and improving both the secular and the religious spheres of activity—a dichotomy that was, in any case, foreign to African culture—was taken for granted by the leading church men and women. Self-help, self-development, and racial advancement in every department of life were assumed to be what Christ meant by the abundant life (John 10:10). Participation in community affairs and cultural development was considered, therefore, to be part of the gospel and the natural responsibility of the church.

Together with survival and elevation, liberation from bondage—the liberation of body and soul from racism, grinding poverty, and all other forms of exploitation and oppression—was the third major concern of black religion

48

in the United States. Nothing has been more successfully demonstrated than the obsession the slaves had with emancipation, or the preoccupation of free blacks with the independence of their indigenous institutions from white control. That is the story of the Prince Hall Masons, the Free African Societies, the black abolitionist movement after the 1840s, and the churches. The well-known text "If the Son makes you free, you will be free indeed [John 8:36]" was taken with utmost seriousness. No amount of equivocation by the white churches could dissuade blacks from believing that God willed freedom for all people. Despite the ever-present threat of violence, antebellum black Christians never doubted that Jesus was a Liberator and that his church was under a mandate to abolish slavery, racial discrimination, and political disfranchisement.

In the light of these historic motifs, black theological reflection began with an affirmation of the inseparability of the personal and the communal, the psychological and spiritual efficacy of religion in sustaining life and sanity in a world of tribulation. The themes of survival, elevation, and liberation also reinforce the corporate and pragmatic function of the church in rolling back the curtain of human degradation to permit the light of freedom and brotherhood/sisterhood to pour into the world. Theological reflection on the black experience cannot conceive of these pillars of the tradition in isolation from one another. They are intimately bound together. Any attempt to place emphasis on one at the expense of the others is to falsify the distinctive character that African American religion has bequeathed to Christian theology.

A Pastoral Critique of the Liberation Emphasis

One of the most consistent criticisms of black theology is that it does not contain a vertical dimension: the profoundly

God-ward aspect of traditional black faith. How justified is such criticism? At least two black theologians, Cecil Cone and Henry Mitchell, would agree that black theology is excessively action-oriented and political, that unless it finds a way to become more inward and address the felt needs and hurts of individuals it will never become a viable option for the masses.[11] Such criticism is difficult to evade. There is no doubt that black theology is in danger of becoming too impersonal, purely theoretical—another political ideology. As such it will certainly be ignored by the majority of both clergy and laity.

In their book entitled *Soul Theology: The Heart of American Black Culture*, Henry H. Mitchell, a black theologian, and Nicholas C. Lewter, a black Baptist pastor and a psychotherapist in private practice, uncover the core belief system of the black church with the purpose of reconstructing what they call our "soul theology." They purport to demonstrate how it is possible to lead people to greater emotional stability, physical well-being, and spiritual wholeness by raising latent folk affirmations to consciousness and encouraging their clients to reappropriate the therapeutic power of black belief. Accordingly, Mitchell and Lewter contend that soul theology, "unlike the widespread classification of Black theology with the theologies of liberation," which they evidently reject, preserves the "nourishing spirituality" of the black folk belief system.[12]

Soul Theology contributes an important corrective to black theological reflection that has sometimes been excessively polemical and exclusively oriented to political action. It rightly brings black religious scholars back to the pastoral dimensions of theology that were neglected in the 1960s. But notwithstanding this virtue, the authors fail to make unambiguously clear that black or soul theology cannot be either-or, but must be both-and. It is precisely the pragmatic spirituality of black faith that ensures that both the personal and the social aspects of our experience must be included in the work of the church. And because the personal and the social realms are inseparable in real life, black or soul theology, properly understood, refuses to make pastoral ministry a personal or spiritual function that can be separated from Christian political action.

My friendly but most serious criticism of Mitchell and Lewter's interpretation of the theological task is that it does not take enough account of the way that personal ills (as C. Wright Mills was fond of saying) inescapably bisect social problems. That conjunction of the personal and the social dimensions is simply taken for granted by mental health practitioners who work in the black community.

During the 1960s two black psychiatrists, William H. Grier and Price M. Cobbs, published a study based on their clinical work with black patients. They examined scores of cases of psychological suffering that required professional counseling. They found that in many instances mental illness was directly traceable to internalized frustration and rage induced by the effects of racism and oppression in the environment.

> One of the problems in understanding the discontent of black people in America is highlighted in this material. The relationship between intrapsychic functioning and the larger social environment is exceedingly complex. Among other things, Negroes want to change inside but find it difficult to do so unless things outside are changed as well.[13]

Price and Cobb present an even more sobering thought. It was their conclusion that the role of the Christian religion, as shaped by white norms and values, had more often served to depreciate and debase black people than to make them more self-esteeming and psychologically healthy.[14] In other words, their data would seem to argue for the necessity of black Christian theology to counteract the negative, guilt-producing effects of the religion that was foisted on blacks during slavery, a form of Christianity that continues to regard blackness symbolically as that which is innately inferior and evil.

I think, however, that both Grier and Price, and Mitchell and Lewter have overstated their cases in opposite directions from each other. A more correct view is that authentic black religion has refused to disengage the spiritual from the secular. The best of black preaching down through the centuries has made it clear that piety and practical action go together, that neither personal counseling nor political action is sufficient to ensure peace of mind and happiness. My childhood pastor, the Rev. Arthur E. Rankin, always reminded us that "you ought to pray about it, but soon you have to get off your knees and *do* something." It was also a familiar saying among some black preachers that I have known that "if you don't do the devil, the devil will sure do you!" These choice examples of folk wisdom tell us that aggressive discipleship in the world, continuous engagement in struggle, is one way of keeping Satan off balance, of defending oneself and one's congregation against the ever-present machinations of evil.

Black ministers have been convinced that only those who know God by personal faith and have been sanctified by the blood of Christ are able to fight off the forces arrayed against them, both in the depths of the psyche and in the external world of tribulation and distress. It is the power of the Holy Spirit in a situation of extreme adversity that refreshes the weary "soldier of the cross" and equips him or her to "stay in the field, children, ah, until the war is ended"; to fight with all your might, both in the physical body and in the body politic.

Incidentally, Dr. King understood this inseverable connection between the experience of the presence of God—the sense of holiness or sanctification—and the struggle for liberation. His ministry recapitulates much of the tumultuous history of black religion's involvement in patching up broken lives for ministry in the world, of bringing wholeness and healing into the context of the struggle for that eschatological kingdom of love and justice, toward which the church works and prays at the same time! An old Negro spiritual expresses what was the overarching theme of King's ministry and of thousands of other black preachers both before and after the Civil War.

> O stay in the field, children-ah
> Stay in the field, children-ah,
> Stay in the field,
> Until the war is ended.
> I've got my breastplate, sword and shield,
> And I'll go marching thro' the field,
> Till the war is ended.

Mitchell and Lewter are to be commended for trying to make black theology more of a pastoral theology. But making it more pastoral should not mean that it must be divested of its theory and praxis as a theology of liberation. Because it cannot speak of wholeness and healing without, at the same time, speaking of health delivery systems, government bureaucracies, social security, houses, and jobs, black theology will not offer people a spiritual bromide for temporary relief. Instead, it seeks to motivate them to work for the political changes that abolish misery and promote *permanent* health for millions. The emphasis on pastoral ministry is, therefore, a welcome improvement, but it must delve more deeply into the historic black response to our Lord's description of ministry that has been a basic text for black ministry: "to set at liberty those who are oppressed [Luke 4:18]."

Black theology must have a pastoral focus but in a different sense than most white pastors understand what that means. It has, for example, been mistakenly assumed by some scholars that what is called pastoral theology is a field of study considerably less demanding than systematic theology or biblical studies. At some seminaries pastoral theology has to do primarily with the "nuts and bolts" of ministry in the local congregation. It sets the theological parameters for "pastoral care and counseling" and the practical parameters for pastoral ministry in terms of such areas as preaching, hymnody, Christian education, church administration, and other things that pastors are supposed to do on a daily basis. But in the black church it is precisely what pastors do on a daily basis that connects the gospel message of personal salvation to the reality of structural unemployment, inadequate welfare checks, teenage pregnancy, personal illness, and public misery. In other words, mobilizing, motivating, and instructing the saints to take charge of their lives by using the church as a battering ram against social problems has been a key aspect of pastoral ministry in the black church.

Thomas C. Oden, a white pastoral theologian, expresses this sense of pastoral theology as an important academic discipline when he writes that it "seeks to join the theoretical with the practical."[15] The point Oden makes is well taken in that he suggests the action-reflection model as a paradigm for pastoral theology. Black pastoral theologians would, however, put greater emphasis and explicitness on leading worship, preaching, and praying as *setting the spiritual or pneumatological context* for the practical, external

response of the congregation to all who suffer from deper-
sonalization and oppression.

Black theology is a form of pastoral theology, therefore,
in quite a specific sense. Not merely because it "deals with
those consequences [of God's self-disclosure in history] as
they pertain to the roles, tasks, duties, and work of the
pastor" (Oden), but also because it draws from scripture,
tradition, culture, and experience that power in congregational worship that unites sanctification and liberation. It
enables the pastor and others who have shepherding responsibilities in the church to bring together personal ills
and social problems, the health-giving experience of spiritual disciplines and the *shalom*-making experience of action in the world for survival, elevation, and liberation.

Black theology, as a pastoral theology, [16] seeks to read the
signs of the times in order to discover what God is doing
both with individuals who are trapped in the maze of
personal sin and with communities that are struggling to be
freed from structures that rob them of peoplehood and self-
determination. Black theologians seek to engender,
through worship, preaching, teaching, and exemplary action in the world, a pragmatic spirituality that takes hold of
broken lives and leads people individually, but also corpo-
rately, into healing conflict with every inauthentic and
unauthorized power over their existence.

Although James H. Cone, a leading exponent of contemporary black theology, does not define what he does ex-
plicitly as a pastoral theology, his writings have consistently
recognized that coherence between black spirituality in the
sanctuary and the struggle for black liberation in the
streets. For Cone, any study of the pilgrimage of our
people from slavery will confirm the inseparability of sanctification and liberation. Thus he stresses the necessary role
of what are considered the basic disciplines of pastoral

theology—worship, preaching, education, and pastoral leadership—in nurturing the souls of black folk and helping their churches to become agents of God's liberation in the world. According to Cone, black Christians have characteristically held these two aspects of ministry together.

> The contradiction between the experience of sanctification and human slavery has always been a dominant theme in black religion. It is found not only in the rise of independent black churches but also in our songs, stories, and sermons. When the meaning of sanctification is formed in the social context of an oppressed community in struggle for liberation, it is difficult to separate the experience of holiness from the spiritual empowerment to change the existing societal arrangements. If "I'm a chile of God wid soul set free" because "Christ hab bought my liberty," then I will find it impossible to tolerate slavery and oppression. [17]

Since the civil rights movement of the 1960s the black church has shown signs of slowly recovering its distinctive features and returning to the rock of survival, elevation, and liberation from whence it was hewn in the eighteenth century. Recent years have seen a return to roots, a revitalization of black culture. Once again black church members, except in the more aristocratic congregations, are expressing themselves with public testimonies during worship, singing spirituals and gospel songs, and using the body as well as the voice in rendering praise to God. For the past decade or more the influence of black Pentecostalism on even the more staid churches has been marked. To be sure, not everyone in African Methodist, Presbyterian, or Episcopal congregations has been happy about it. Nevertheless, most people have been open to the "old-time religion" and quite ready to explore the rich cultural matrix of African American spirituality that sustained so many previous generations against anomie and dehumanization. If there has been any problem, it has been the problem of persuading these people that what they are dredging out of the past is not some facsimile of white evangelical Protestantism, but a distinctive black theology that achieved maturity in the nineteenth century and made the church a powerful cultural as well as spiritual institution.

It has not been easy to help black Christians move beyond the surface features of the "old-time religion" to its more profoundly social and political meanings. Contemporary black theology, in its activist or political modality, has suffered from suspicion and misunderstanding among both clergy and laity. That is why it is necessary to emphasize its function as a pastoral theology in the older tradition, but only if we correctly perceive what that tradition was like.

We need to be constantly reminded that the "old-time religion" had a powerful, if often covert, social action and cultural renewal component that was utilized by our predecessors in church schools, lyceums, literary societies, benevolence clubs, and abolitionist groups *within* the congregations. Participation in such activities was substantive evidence of being "entirely saved," and members of a saving community. This weekday life and work of the city churches contributed inestimably to the well-being and psychological stamina of their members and of the community at large. The point needs to be made over and over, in the face of many temptations today to retreat into an anti-intellectualism, privatism, and mystical other-worldliness, that for our ancestors—even as late as the turn of the century—true spirituality was considered to be neither unreflective nor devoid of social relevance. Being born again, sanctified and praising "the Lord" in private life, was a prerequisite to the proper exercise of cultural and political responsibility during the antislavery crusade, in the

Reconstruction, and throughout the anticolonial and pan-African struggle of the churches in the early twentieth century.

Whether or not our black churches will be able to build for the future on this rich inheritance depends on their current leadership. The relatively newer denominations from the Holiness and Pentecostal families will have to assume a larger responsibility for teaching the faith in a way that meets the continuing needs of black and other oppressed minorities. At the same time, the older denominations that helped to shape the original tradition must become more sensitive to the current deficiencies of black theology, including its excessive activism and its debilitating sexism that has not yet fully recognized and embraced the contribution of black women to liberation.

If black theologians will acknowledge that struggle against social injustice is a necessary, but not sufficient concern of theological reflection, they will help to close the current gap between the so-called mainstream and the more evangelical churches. That gap can be reduced by reconceptualizing the pastoral function of black theology and giving more assistance to local congregations for the development of more holistic ministries that heal the body as well as the soul.

The Challenge to the White Churches

I come now to the third question that is being asked of black theologians today. Is black theology so narrowly focused on the black condition in the United States that it loses any relevance for people who are not black? This is another way of asking whether this way of doing theology is compatible with the main currents of the historical stream of orthodoxy that has flowed from the West and, in virtue of such compatibility, has something significant to contribute to the ecumenical movement and the world mission of the church.

Sydney E. Ahlstrom, a celebrated American church historian, made a remark about black religious history that might well be applied to the field of systematic theology. Ahlstrom observed the desirability of a "thorough renovation" of American church history.[18] He went on to suggest that the paradigm for such a renovation is the black religious experience that had been excluded from all previous synoptic histories of Christianity in the Western hemisphere. With the same concern for recovering hitherto discarded traditions that radically challenge the norms of the majority, it can be argued that black theology provides a paradigm for the renovation of American systematic theology. Indeed, it is not unreasonable to assume that because black theology is correcting its deficiencies and becoming more open to wider criticism and reform from other Third World theologies, this first indigenous liberation theology in North America is already making a constructive contribution to the emerging theological consensus of world Christianity. What challenge does this development present to the predominantly white churches of the United States, and what does it promise for the future?

The context for the consideration of such a question is what many regard as the current revival of conservative Christianity. As far as the United States and many of the nations of the Caribbean basin are concerned, the recent and widely publicized success of the "Protestant evangelical revolution" has brought mixed blessings. On the one hand, the dead hand of theological liberalism has been raised from the wellspring of religious revival, and a flood of evangelical faith is bursting forth from masses of people who had been reached by neither conservative Roman

Catholicism nor the old-line Protestant churches of the United States and Canada. Not the least responsible for this revival of "old-time religion" in the heartland of North America and its satellite countries south of the border has been the skillful utilization of mass media, particularly television, by evangelistic preachers whose knowledge of the Bible is no less developed than their knowledge of sharp business practices. On the other hand, the upsurge of born-again religiosity, which has the strong flavor of the bourgeoisification of previously repressed populations, has shown little inclination to defend the human rights these people were previously denied and to oppose the obvious excesses and injustices of monopoly capitalism. Indeed, the new fundamentalism is politically reactionary, so moralistic as to be ready to suppress any dissent from its own ideas of virtue, opposed to cultural pluralism and secular humanism, and hysterically anti-Communist. Ecumenical Christians cannot help but ask themselves, Is this what was heralded fifty years ago as "the Christian century"? Is this what is called the triumph of the gospel in the modern world?

Although the black church has not been invulnerable to enticements from the Christian right, it has not suffered a loss of membership to conservative churches to the extent that the older white denominations have, nor has it been similarly inclined to pull in its horns and become theologically fainthearted in order to deflect criticism from the new born-again preachers. The theological tradition of black Christianity in the United States has been both pragmatic and spiritual. It has always been oriented to human liberation and ready to do battle with any interpretation of the faith that either removes it from politics altogether, or strikes an alliance with political and economic conservatism. Although the black church has seldom been tempted by communism, it has never bought into the periodic anti-Communist crusades of the Bible Belt, or rejected out of hand the Marxist critique of religion and capitalism. Black theology, which represents this tough but resilient tradition, is a prime candidate for the renovation of the embattled ecumenical theology of the mainstream denominations in the United States at this point in history.

Nothing is more urgently needed than such a renovation in this period when the Jimmy Swaggarts, Jerry Falwells, and Pat Robertsons are having phenomenal success with their appeals to the white middle class for retrenchment from social legislation dealing with domestic poverty, for American intervention in Central America, and for a summary rejection of liberation theology. A popular Pentecostal minister in Atlanta whose congregation of almost ten thousand members includes many middle-class Negroes offers what he calls a "kingdom theology." In an interview with an *Atlanta Constitution* reporter he is alleged to have said: "It is a whole new theology. . . . What we're doing is setting up a network by which we can spread propaganda. . . . We will accomplish enough [so] that the systems of the world will collapse because of their inability to survive, and what will be left will be a system the church has built."[19]

The kingdom theology of the conservative evangelicals intends to institute infallible Christian politics, Christian economics, Christian public education, and a Christian culture that "will take dominion over the world." It would snatch us all, beginning in the United States, the Caribbean, and Central America, from the jaws of the secular humanists, the gay community, and Godless communism. It need not be concerned with poverty and degradation because it teaches that the poor and oppressed are God-forsaken because of their sins. It has no use for the World Council or the National Council of Churches because these abhorrent agencies of Satan support contextual theologies and approve of cultural pluralism.

It should come as no surprise that black theologians belong to an ethnic community that has long experienced racism at the hands of religious people who characteristically make such claims. We suspect that the old-fashioned evangelical revolution of today frequently masks an old-fashioned white supremacy. Therein lies one answer to our question regarding the broader implications of black theology. Black theology has to do with more than the black church because it contributes to the enlightenment of white Christians by unmasking the racism and cultural imperialism that lurks under the outer garments of this new fundamentalism. In its best form, therefore, black theology presents a theological option for the poor and oppressed that can help the American churches recover a compassionate and holistic pastoral ministry that recognizes an essential coherence between the biblical concept of authentic spirituality and liberal politics.

The Dutch theologian Theo Witvliet writes about black theology as representative of the underside of history where Christ is and where the church must also be.

> The confrontation with black theology here represents an enormous positive challenge. Its polemic has a positive side, "Polemic is love." In its unmasking of the contradiction of Christianity there is a plea for conversion, *metanoia*, for a radical transformation of perspective, which leads to the domain of the hidden history, the history which, judged by the usual church norms, belongs rather in the history of heresy. Black theology wants to argue from this specific history extending from the invisible church of the time of slavery [that in this history] there is a glimpse of liberation, of the great light that shines over those who live in a land of deep darkness (Isaiah 9:1; John 1:5).[20]

Although he was grossly misunderstood when he first made the statement, James H. Cone was on sound ground when he wrote in 1969 that white Christians have to become black. "To be black," he wrote, "means that your heart, your soul, your mind, and your body are where the dispossessed are."21 Many whites were incensed that anyone would dare suggest that they had to become black in order to be born again. But Cone was saying that insofar as blackness in the color symbolism of all Western societies stands for the "despised and rejected of men," God is black, Jesus is the black messiah, and no one can be reconciled to the least of Christ's brothers and sisters without taking up the reproach of blackness, that is, identification with the oppressed and participation in their struggle for humanity and liberation.

Witvliet puts it as helpfully as anyone I know, substantially supporting the argument that black theology is not only for black Christians, but has something to offer other Christians as well. He writes:

> Black history confronts theology with a fundamental epistemological insight: God's otherness or exteriority ("the vertical from above") is not a theological metaphysic but is indissolubly connected with the fate and struggle of those for whom there is no place in his world. Their otherness represents his otherness. And in a society which is dominated by the conflict between white and black, this means that God is black.22

It may not be necessary for white Christians to become so explicit about the "color of God," but the point ought not to be missed that a thoughtful appropriation of black theological concepts should help white pastors and church leaders to identify with "the wretched of the earth," to deprogram white middle-class Christians who have become accustomed to picture Jesus as a long-haired, blond suburbanite with a beautiful tan, who vindicates their most pious pretentions and their obsession with white power over "lesser breeds without the law."

Second, white American Christians can learn from black theology that pastoral care and counseling must not only bring "the peace that passeth understanding," but must also redirect people to the *missio Dei,* to God's work of liberation and reconciliation in the world. Black people are certainly not the only people in bondage in America. The white churches need to help their people experience the power of the Holy Spirit in black worship that not only renders a psychosomatic liberty superior to what most patients find on the psychiatrist's couch, but, as Dr. King's movement demonstrated, can also march them down the aisle joyously singing the songs of Zion and into the highways and byways to unbind the world from the demons of injustice and oppression.

The immediate challenge of black theology to the ecumenical movement is to make white churches consider an option for Christian faith and action of which they have been previously unaware. It challenges white pastors and congregations once again to seek *koinonia* and cooperation with their black counterparts in the same community or metropolitan area—to come out of the foxholes of affluence and privilege and discover another American religious tradition that may surprise us with some new remedies for the brokenness of the Body of Christ and impel us into the world together. Is it too much to expect the National Council of Churches to be bold enough to lead the "blackenization" of American theology to this end?

Finally, the world mission of the church, which was so notably influenced by the Montgomery bus boycott and the religiously motivated, nonviolent civil rights movement in the United States, can be reinvigorated by drawing certain insights about spirituality and struggle from the black theology movement. James H. Cone contends that black theology is modest in its claim to have the truth and, by respecting the "pre-reflective visions of the poor as defined by their political struggles" everywhere in the world, opens itself to revelations of God's will and purpose from religions other than Christianity.[23] In a world that has almost become a single neighborhood the ecumenical movement needs to be instructed by such a theological perspective. Theological absolutism is not only counterproductive for world development and peace, but also contrary to the most profound meaning of the religion of Jesus. Black Christians have always been wary of people who rush to judgment about what is right and what is wrong; of dogmatic confessions of faith and churches that are so proud of their doctrinal purity that they cannot imagine any imperfection in their social policies and practices. Only when one has been lowered into the depths of suffering and powerlessness does one give up illusions about infallibility and perfectibility; only when one must cry out with Jesus, "My God, why hast thou forsaken me?" does it seem right, good, and a gift of grace to be able to seize upon the truth that consoles and frees wherever it may be found. Such openness to other truth is a basic characteristic of African religions that is still residual in African American religion. The world mission of the church is called today to openness, dialogue, and collaboration with other faiths and ideologies, particularly in the Third World, where the gifts that God has given to other races and nationalities have been deprecated and submerged by a triumphant Euro-American religion and civilization. Because most of those other races and nationalities are people of color, black theology is more empathetic with pilgrims on other paths to God, and therefore has something to teach the ecumenical movement about Christian tolerance.

Yet, as Cone reminds us, black theology remains unswervingly committed to Jesus, the incarnate Son of God, and (as it attempts, nevertheless, to overcome its sexism) points to a belief and way of life that is rooted and grounded in scripture and in an experience of the Holy Spirit, who comes to us in the throes of suffering and struggle.

It is the knowledge that we belong *only* to God that enables black Christians to keep on fighting for justice even though the odds might be against us. We firmly believe that Jesus heals wounded spirits and broken hearts. No matter what trials and tribulations blacks encounter, we refuse to let despair define our humanity. We simply believe that "God can make a way out of no way."[24]

Conclusion

I have attempted to present black theology as a perspective on the Christian faith from the underside of history that has important implications for pastoral ministry—in white churches as well as in black. The implications that I have discussed, however, know nothing of the radical disjunction between the sacred and the profane, personal piety and political witness, the ministry of counseling room and the ministry of the sidewalks that has sometimes characterized white fundamentalism and a conservative posture on pastoral ministry.

During the past twenty-five years black theology has been, in part, a pastoral response to what W.E.B. DuBois saw as a permanent crisis in African American life in the twentieth century. I have tried to indicate that it also has been a critical response to what I refer to as the pragmatic spirituality of black religion in the United States. More than any other theological movement in this country, even antedating the white social gospel movement, an unsystematized but distinctively cognitive black theological thought brought together the sanctuary and the streets for the salvation of both people and institutions through the lordship of Jesus Christ. The new black theology, building on that illustrious tradition, offers to American religion and the worldwide ecumenical movement a third alternative between an imperious and sanctimonious conservatism on the right and an ambivalent and ineffective liberalism on the left. It is, by no means, a flawless interpretation of the religion of Jesus. But it has something important to contribute to the renewal and solidarity of both black and white Christians in the United States and to the mission and unity of the whole church of Jesus Christ. And judging from what we are reading these days in the daily newspapers and seeing on Sunday morning television, it may be the best that anyone has to offer at this point in the history of Christianity in the United States of America.

CHAPTER 3

Values and Hazards of Theological Preaching

Will D. Campbell

THEOLOGICAL PREACHING? NEVER THOUGHT ABOUT IT! If I did think about it, the thought pattern was a garbled montage. Words like uppity, doctrinal, creedal, ethereal— who the Sam Hill thinks about it.

If we take the word theological in the classic sense— study or knowledge of God—I am fearful to begin thinking about it now. How does one *study* God? And is it not a presumption to assert that we have *knowledge* of God? I have so little *knowledge* of God that it strikes me as a sacrilege to claim any at all.

But now that I have committed myself not only to think theological thoughts, but also to write them down, I must overcome the timidity and begin. Though still jarred. I am

Will D. Campbell, B.D., is a popular author who lives in Mt. Juliet, Tennessee. He is a regular columnist for *Christianity and Crisis*.

a sculptor. I make things. I dream them up. I am the architect. I design plans and then I create something. I take the manifold and rocker arms from an abandoned Allis-Chalmers C Model tractor, weld them together to fashion a cross, fasten that to a stand that was the oil pan, and give the piece of sculpture a name. I call it *The General Confession*. "We acknowledge and bewail our *manifold* sins and wickedness . . ." (That's from the 1928 *Book of Common Prayer*. I haven't bothered to check the newest new one.) I take a big earth auger and five drill bits ranging in size from two feet to a few inches and weld them in a zigzag pattern reaching twelve feet in the air. I name this piece of sculpture *Tower of Babel*. It represents sin in my mind. I take a rusty old farm pump and place it in concrete so that it seems to flow into a large sugar pot filled with water and goldfish. It is, of course, *The Fountain of Life*.

So without really meaning to do so I have constructed a theological system. There is sin, confession, and redemption. All these can be found beyond and behind the little log house that is my office. (I suppose real preachers would call it a study.) I tell you about them for several reasons.

First, these icons suggest the inevitability of theology.

Second, most—and perhaps the best—theological systems come about without the intention of really meaning to create them. Those who create them generally don't take them as seriously as the generations that follow. And sometimes the creators are not aware of what they are doing. I was not aware of what I had done until a young friend exclaimed, "My God, you have your whole belief system here in three pieces of junk!"

In the third place—and most important in my mind—I tell you about them because they represent the presumption and foolishness of theologizing. You see, I said I was the architect, as well as the builder, the creator, of the

69

sculptures. I made them and they are mine. I am their god. I know everything about them. Do they, can they, know anything about me? Do they even *need* to know anything about me? And what would I do if I discovered that they were even *trying* to learn something about me. *Studying* me? You, *thing*, desire knowledge of me? I'll tell you one thing, those objects would be in a heap of trouble. Just as Adam and Eve were in a heap of trouble when they "theologized," when they sought to have "knowledge of God." They were not equipped to deal with knowledge of good and evil.

I suspect that any description or definition a group of pastors would make of God would include something about God as creator, or first cause. Then I expect we would add that the creation of human beings is in no way comparable to my creation of iron sculpture. But can we be sure? What is the criterion for such an assertion? Is it that my statues do not have life? Is it true that they do not have life? Are the stable configurations of atomic nuclei and electrons bound together by electrostatic and electromagnetic forces with predictable behavior life? What *is* life? Once when a woman told Jesus that if he had been there her brother would not have died, he replied, "I am life." Certainly non-Christians would refute that statement and most Christians would qualify it. Yet I recently heard a well-known scholar and educator, Prof. Ivan Illich, affirm it. He was addressing a group that had assembled to discuss whether or not those who oppose the death penalty, those who oppose abortion, and those who oppose nuclear proliferation might possibly be kissing cousins. When asked to begin the proceedings with a prayer he exclaimed, "Not a prayer, but a curse. To hell with life!" Then the sage professor unfolded to the astonished audience the manner in which we Americans have made an idol and called it *life*.

70

I don't know if my statues have life or not. I do know that they do not always behave as I wish. They rust, decay, change colors, fall down. But, you say, they have no brain, no motor skills. Very well. I can fix that. I gave them motor skills. I tied a large magnet to the *General Confession*. The idea was that as the wind blew the *Tower of Babel*, causing it to sway in the direction of the manifold cross, the magnet would bring it within its influence, draw it closer, and then release its grasp when the wind subsided, making it move with regularity, like the little duck one sees in truck stops and souvenir shops that constantly dips its beak into a glass of water. The motor worked all right, but a weakly welded joint gave way, and the top half of the tower came tumbling to the ground. That invert metaphor suggests that sometimes it is our brain, our very *theology*, that gets us into trouble.

And that leads us back to the subject at hand. Or at least to part of the subject—the hazards of theological preaching. On one occasion, when a certain prophecy didn't come to pass, Jeremiah observed that it is not good to be too sure of God. On the one hand, it is permissible and appropriate for one's religion to be dogmatic, even doctrinaire. Without some degree of sureness it isn't worth much. But on the other hand, even a cursory reading of Jewish and Christian scripture reveals more faith than certainty. Consider Abraham, going out by faith, not knowing whither he went. Consider the prophets. Consider the apostle Paul, who, toward the end of his life, was plagued with the thought that after having preached to others, he missed the way himself. And consider Jesus pleading for the passing of the bitter cup, asking if there were not some other way. All of them had doubts and questions.

Today we are bombarded with a theology of certainty. Not just from the electronic soul-molesters whose satellites hurl to hearth and household a gospel of take up your cross and relax; take up your cross and find self-esteem in an edifice made of glass; take up your cross and get rich or become President. Not just from biblical theme parks and the world's largest wave pool. Not just from Texas judges and rich Dallas preachers who sometimes appear to read only until their lips get tired and with that authority go out to take over one of the nation's largest religious bodies, seeking to make robots of its adherents and eunuchs, and handmaidens of its scholars and teachers.

And to give balance, not just from the great Church of Rome, whose logic on who may or may not be a priest seems to be based on the fact that none of Jesus' apostles were female, while by that same logic *no* Gentiles of either sex could be ordained priest because none of Jesus' apostles were Gentiles.

To keep that in proportion I must also point out that my Holy Mother Church, the Southern Baptist Convention, under the influence cited above, resolved three years ago that women should not be ordained because man was first in creation and woman was first in the Edenic fall. By that logic it seems to me that women should be given the advantage in the right to ordination on the basis that they discovered sin first, have been at it longer, and thus should be more adept at identifying sin and casting it out. But then logic generally does not prevail over bigotry.

Yes, the theology of certitude can be found in those places. But now its influence is felt and the rhetoric spoken at the highest level of government. I have no problem with my neighbors gathering on Sunday mornings and believing that the earth is flat, that it was created on Central Standard time by a digital watch, that it is five thousand years old, and that the Antichrist, whose full name is Secular Humanism, speaks Russian. I begin to have problems, however, when I realize that those things are becoming the national agenda and that their validity is decided in Caesar's courtrooms.

I feel no discomfort if one comes to my yard and wants to talk to me about being born again. It is when I hear it as a criterion for citizenship or public leadership that I am disquieted. I must raise some questions if Caesar is going to get into the business of born again. I can trust God with that—however I might define and describe God. I do not, cannot, trust Caesar with it.

I must ask, is it true that you're going to be born again by prostrating yourself, repenting, following some personal stylistic rules? Does it work? Yes. It works for minor and non-sins—gossiping, drinking liquor, gambling, and the like.

Does it work on peace? Apparently it does not, for its most vocal advocates are continually calling for more, bigger, better instruments of war. Nay, instruments of destruction, for the nuclear bombs are not weapons of war. They are tools of annihilation. They defend us from nothing.

Does it work on justice? I hear little talk of justice within the ranks of Caesar's born-again kingdom. I see little evidence of it.

The biggest thing it doesn't work on is children. The born-againism of both Caesar and religion, now rapidly becoming the same thing, will constrain us, and our children, to be nice to fellow church members, not to steal apples from the other kids' lunch bags, and maybe even not to use dangerous drugs. But it won't constrain you to be livid about a world order that permits nationalism to flourish and an economic world order that encourages, and in places makes necessary, the flow of drugs to our streets. Nor will it constrain us to be livid about the kind of global nationalism that threatens to make annihilation of the children inevitable. Why, in the name of God, or the name of anyone, can't there be a simple, one-sentence peace treaty that all nations would readily subscribe to: *It shall be a violation of international law for one nation to kill the children of another in time of war.* That would stop it because all our tools of destruction are designed to annihilate everyone. None of them can distinguish between my grandson and Oliver North. And even our own conventional weapons apparently cannot distinguish between Omar Qaddafi and his children.

Does it work at the level of love? Apparently not. In the sixteenth century a little band of radical Christians demonstrated love by refusing to bear arms for church or state, would not serve on juries to judge another human being, vehemently opposed the death penalty. And these left-wingers, the Anabaptists, were drowned in the Amstel River like rats, were tied on ladders and pushed into burning brush heaps, were hunted by armed horsemen like rabbits. Last summer forty-five thousand of their descendants, who seem to spend more time blow-drying their hair than thinking or studying about their heritage, moved into Atlanta with more hate than one can find this side of the Near East, breathing fire over the alleged inerrancy of a manuscript that they all admit no one has ever seen.

In partial preparation for this essay, I gave a video cassette of Jerry Falwell, Jimmy Swaggart, Pat Robertson, Ernest Angley, and Jim Bakker to Tom T. Hall, a country picker, storyteller, novelist, philosopher, friend, and neighbor. I asked him to view the tape straight through and give me a bottom-line appraisal of what he had seen. He called on Monday morning with his report: "My God can whip your God." That is, to be sure, a theological statement. But it is a dangerous theological statement.

But wait a minute! Is it possible that *all* theological

statements are dangerous? Potentially explosive and violent? Where did the notions I have been describing come from? How do they differ essentially from our own notions? What are Falwell and Robertson trying to do that Calvin and Luther did not try to do? We might argue that Calvin advocated a religious commonwealth, and not a theocracy, but I'm not sure we can draw that line. However, please note that at this point I am asking questions, not attempting to answer them. So I continue to ask them. What is the difference between the First Mainline Church by the Bank and the 700 Club? To ask it more harshly, what's the difference between Oral Roberts' Tower of Power and the Pope's jewels? Certainly we can make a qualitative distinction between the beauty of the Sistine Chapel and the crassness of a satellite. But as we do, should we not try to be sure we are not drawing lines of sophistication, lines of elitism? It is permissible for the governors and managers to build that which is aesthetically pleasing to us, but it is unacceptable for the pulpwood haulers, the plebians, to contribute their collective offerings to build what is aesthetically pleasing to them. Whatever else we might say, on this we can agree: The price of all these things can be traced to the backs of the poor. Great fortunes are made from men, women, and children going into mines, fields, and mills. Whether or not we can establish a theological, cultural, or qualitative difference, all of us, at one time or another, have sung the song "Praise the Lord, and Send Me the Money."

Whether we can distinguish between St. John's by the Bank and the electronic church is not our task. Our task is to talk of the hazards and values of theological preaching. The main thing that makes me fearful of theology, and thus theological preaching, is that theology so often leads to violence. Nothing is so dangerous as religion when it gets

75

out of hand. When it got out of hand, and slingshots and hand-cast spears were the weapons for settling disagreements, it wasn't so bad. But that day is surely gone forever. No longer is it David against Goliath, Ephrathites against Philistines. Today we talk of settling our differences, even religious differences, with nuclear weapons. Too often we use a theology designed for slingshots and spears and apply it to a nuclear age.

Let's do a quick review of that theology and its roots. And even to use the word theology we must use it relative to something. We must begin with some vague notion of what it is of which we are seeking knowledge. Which God do we want to study and preach about? By now you have probably guessed that the only God I can talk about is one of great mystery, of awe and wonderment, one of whom I claim to know very little. Ask me what I mean when I say, "God," and I will tell you that is what I mean. God is God is God is God is God and then a period. Or if one wants to be daring and go farther, maybe add a semicolon. Or no punctuation at all. Extremely dangerous, it seems to me.

We think of Moses. He's out looking for the cattle and stumbles on what he might have thought was some fox-hunter's campfire. When he gets a bit closer he sees that it is a bush on fire. Not terribly exciting, but generally a bush on fire is quickly consumed. This one isn't. It just goes on burning. Not only that, it begins to speak, to give instructions. Go here, talk to this group of folks, tell them thus and so. Moses was probably mildly daunted by both developments. But he just said, "Okay. All right." Then something jolted him. Hold on. What if they ask me who sent me. Who are you? What do I say? What is my *authority* for saying these things? What do I do then? And the voice said, "Just tell them I AM has sent you." And Moses, never one to get too excited but moderately agitated by then, exclaimed, "Holy Moses!" Or something like that. "Now Mr. I AM, I can't tell them that. They'll think I'm out of my gourd. They'll make me take Thorazine. Send me down to Houston for counseling. Already I have to go for speech therapy. You gotta be kidding." And then, being in fox-hunting country and familiar with the vernacular, added, "No, it's time to pee on the fire, call the dogs, and go to the house. This hunt is over."

"No. No, no," the voice said. "Just tell them I AM WHO I AM sent you."

And so it began. Theological preaching is talking to folks about somebody called I AM and applying it to something we call *life*. And I have already said that I know little about what *life* is. And when someone asks me what I mean by the word life, I just say, "Life is WOW!!" So we try—or I try—to talk about something so mysterious as to be called I AM. And we can't. So we—or I—try to talk "in the spirit" of the inscrutable and apply it to something equally inscrutable called "life."

Well, I seem to have adopted a resource book. We call it the Bible. And what is the *Bible?* We have been told before and apparently now need telling again: the Bible is a book about who God is. It is not a book about salvation, love, justice, peace—certainly not a book about peace, for it is filled with violence. I make no apology for using it as a resource book for that is what it is. Only now the authority of the Bible is under serious, if not lethal, attack. From inerrantists and from literalists. As for the inerrantists, to swear that we believe to be inerrant a manuscript no one has ever seen, and thus cannot know what it says, would be laughable, except that idolatry is never funny. But the world does laugh, and the authority of the Bible is trivialized. And certainly no one takes the Bible literally. No one! A man came to our place not long ago and, based on some of the things he said in our conversation, I gathered that he thought he did. So I asked him: "Do you believe the Bible literally?"

"Yes sir! Word for word. Just the way it is written."

"Well, good for you," I said, extending one hand and reaching for his hat with the other. "I do too. I didn't know there was another person in the world who agreed with me. So come on. I've been waiting for you. I have a little project over in West Nashville I need some help with. Jesus said he had come to set the prisoners free. I can't tear that damn penitentiary down by myself and now I have some help. Let's go."

"Now, what Jesus *meant* by that was . . ."

"No, no, no! Don't start exegeting on me. You said you believed exactly what the Bible says and that's what it says. Are you coming with me or not?" Well, the penitentiary is still standing.

Whatever value there may be in theological preaching— and I seem to wander from value to hazard with abandon— surely part of it is to establish what the Bible is. And how the devil must cheer at the success of those who make it an idol.

And in talking about it we cannot shy away from the violence it contains. You know as well as I that violence comes early in the Bible and remains until Revelation is winding down. The story has barely begun when a fellow kills his own blood *brother.* I can't think of a worse form of violence. And as the story is ending, a rider with flaming eyes and a sword in his mouth to smite the nations is paraded past the reader.

At an early age we learned of violence in Sunday school. And from preachers. How we cheered as we watched a little runt named David kill "The Fridge."

Saul hath slain his thousands,
and David his ten thousands.
—1 Samuel 18:7

Slain! What did it mean when this peewee running back,
before the charge, said to Goliath: "I have come against you
in the name of the Lord of hosts, the God of the army of
Israel, which you have defied. The Lord will put you into
my power this day; I will kill you and cut your head off and
leave your carcass and the carcasses of the Philistines to the
birds and the wild beasts; all the world shall know that
there is a God in Israel" (see 1 Samuel 17:45–46). A God of
violent deeds. The story as told in a country Sunday school
class by Aunt Donie seemed harmless enough. But put it in
the hands of a presidential candidate who on command can
redirect the appointed route of a hurricane and who in the
name of the same God that David was following calls for
more, not fewer, more powerful, not less powerful, nuclear
exterminators to stop the march of atheistic communism or
secular humanism and I am frightened.

We heard the wild anthem of praise of Moses' sister
Miriam as Pharaoh's army drowns in the sea: "Sing ye to
the Lord, for he hath triumphed gloriously; the horse and
his rider hath he thrown into the sea [Exod. 15:21, KJV]."

We heard the stories told and romanticized. As youngsters we were galvanized by the account of Jael and Sisera
in the book of Judges. We lived down close to the Louisiana
line, close to the Bayou country, and Aunt Donie thought
Jael was a Cajun. A cheerleader for the Ragin' Cajuns down
at what used to be Southwestern Louisiana Institute in
LaFayette. You remember the story. Deborah had sent
Barak out to fight the Canaanites, heavily outnumbered.
But Barak had put them to rout. And Sisera, the command-

ing officer of the Canaanite forces, did what a lot of head officers do when the troops are taking a licking. He got his corncob pipe and braided cap and said, "I shall return." He bailed out. Now Aunt Donie suspected that Sisera was somehow acquainted with Jael already. In fact she found a billet-doux (love letter) in his pocket. In any case he made his way to her tent. In telling the story Aunt Donie would skip prissily around the Sunday school room (actually just part of the main church house with muslin curtains stretched across some clothesline wire to make a little enclosure. We didn't have but just the one room). Anyway, Aunt Donie would roll her eyes, turn around, and shake her geriatic bootie.

"Hey, big boy. Come on over to my tent, dar. I'm gon' tu give you sometin' lik' you ain't never had before, me." Well, General Sisera, crusty old regular army man that he was, thought he had already had everything you could catch except leprosy. But he went in the tent. And he said, "Now baby, I'm pretty washed out right now, but I tell you what. Let me take a nap and rest up a little and then we'll see." Well, that was all right with Jael because she had a headache anyhow. And her own agenda was not what the egotistical general thought it was. So she covered him up with an old blanket she had bought at the army surplus store, stuffed one of her husband's old T-shirts—the one that said "Caesar's Palace—Gomorrah"—under his head. Rubbed his back, gave him a drink of buttermilk, and told him to get some rest. Said she would wait outside the tent and tell anyone who inquired that he wasn't there. (Deception in the name of God goes way back you see.)

When he started snoring Jael took a ball peen hammer and a long tent peg and drove it through his eardrum. And the Holy Bible tells us that his brains oozed out on the ground, his arms and legs twitched and spasmed, and he died. This pretty little cheerleader had nailed that booger to the ground. In the name of God.

And we all grew quiet and attentive, knowing that all night we would toss and turn with the image of that big general lying there with a number eighty spike driven through his sweetbreads, as Aunt Donie read that beautiful song of Deborah (Judges 5:2, 24–28, 31, NEB):

> For the leaders, the leaders in Israel,
> for the people who answered the call,
> bless ye the Lord.

* * * *

> Blest above women be Jael, . . .
> blest above all women in the tents.
> He asked for water: she gave him milk,
> she offered him curds in a bowl fit for a chieftain.
> She stretched out her hand for the tent-peg,
> her right hand to hammer the weary.
> With the hammer she struck Sisera, she crushed his head;
> she struck and his brains ebbed out.
> At her feet he sank down, he fell, he lay;
> at her feet he sank down and fell.
> Where he sank down, there he fell, done to death.

There was no question in anyone's mind where our sympathies lay. Yet we could sense a kind of motherly empathy as Aunt Donie continued, a kind of worried look on her face:

> The mother of Sisera peered through the lattice,
> through the window she peered and shrilly cried,
> "Why are his chariots so long coming?
> Why is the clatter of his chariots so long delayed?"

You see, Aunt Donie had lost a son in World War I. But she went on:

81

So perish all thine enemies, O Lord;
but let all who love thee be like the sun rising
in strength.

And then she would read the last verse of Judges 5 without comment. I guess I am glad now that she never tried to explain it. After all the gory details the Sunday school lesson ended with these words:

The land was at peace for forty years.

Those words always bothered me. After all the carnage, the slaughter, the suffering, there was peace. Is war necessary for peace? Not in our league. For the years after a nuclear war would not be forty. More like 40 million.

The list of biblical violence is long and all of you know it as well as I. The cities taken over under Joshua, slaughter of all people, destruction of property. In the Judges where the person with the charisma goes beyond. As with Gideon— after he has subdued the kings he continues to chase one of them and kills him; takes power given to him and uses it for revenge. Yes, the Bible is a violent book.

Now, of course, those of us of the Christian tradition like to think that there was a sharp reversal of direction and practice between Malachi and Matthew. This despite the fact that Jesus said he had come not to bring peace, but a sword. Yet the history of the Christian movement is quite as bloody as the history of Israel. And theological preaching has to deal with it. And we have to give answer to those we call the "evangelical right" who, happily with First Amendment protection, embrace, espouse, and appropriate Old Testament proof texts and apply them to contemporary political issues.

We must also deal honestly and boldly with the mischief wrought from our creedal messianism. We cannot deny the blood shed because of this doctrine. We cannot deny the blatant anti-Semitism that continues to fly under this banner. Exactly who Christ was and is continues to be the tough one. CHRIST IS THE ANSWER. We affirm it and put it on Cadillac bumpers. Is that itself not the old dualism? The we/them. If the world is ruled by two antagonistic forces, good and evil, we assume that *we* are the advocates, custodians, practitioners, and defenders of the good and that *they* (whoever the *they* may be) are the advocates and exponents of evil. We can justify anything under the sun, for this is an awesome responsibility.

Would not a better slogan be: Christ lived the answer, showed us the answer, and it was so radical that we did all we knew how to do—we killed him. If Christ *is* the answer, license is a by-product, license rooted in dependency. Christ showed the answer, lived the answer, leads to discipleship, to developing of the potential we all have, to righteousness, to "Be ye perfect," as he, whoever we might think he was, told us to do.

In an important but little-known book called *Witness to The Truth*, Edith Hamilton, a scholar best known for her work in Antiquities, made a statement in 1948 that addresses our subject in a fine fashion.

So the great Church of Christ came into being by ignoring the life of Christ. . . . The Fathers of the church were good men, often saintly men, sometimes men who cared enough for Christ to die for him, but they did not trust him. They could not trust the safety of his church to his way of doing things.

So they set out to make the church safe in their own way. Creeds and theologies protected it from individual vagaries; riches and power [protected it] against outside attacks.

The church was safe. But one thing its ardent builders and defenders failed to see. Nothing that lives can be safe.

Life means danger. The more the church was hedged about with Confessions of Faith and defended by the mighty of the earth, the feebler its life grew.[1]

What this wise woman was saying, it seems to me, or is saying to us in our current context, is what I tried to say earlier: all theological statements, all creeds are potentially dangerous—theology become the enemy of Theology. The management mode, leading in our day to media management mode, came early. Christianity would never be made to work efficiently by following Christ literally, Edith Hamilton said. "He had no methods people could adopt and put to definite use." He never laid down that matter of fundamental importance to an organization, clearly formulated conditions on which one could enter it. He never demanded of the people who wanted to follow him that they must first know this or that, the nature of the Trinity or the plan of salvation. He had not insisted on conviction of sin or consciousness of forgiveness or on any belief whatsoever. He talked of such things as a cup of cold water. Ah, but we must build a global sprinkler system.

But you could not build a steeple on that any more than you can build one on the notion of unconditional grace. So enter creeds and theologies to contain, to systematize. Enter violence to protect and propagate the creeds and theologies. Enter Augustine, Luther, Calvin, Pat Robertson. Jesus did say, "Love your enemies, bless them that curse you, do good to them that hate you, and pray for them which despitefully use you, and persecute you [Matt. 5:44, KJV]." In defense of church and doctrine the great Luther said of the Anabaptists, "They should be put to death." And they were. Among other reasons he listed were that, one, they had no definite doctrine and, two, they suppressed true doctrine. It was *doctrine*, you see, that was paramount and had to be defended, not the *Way* of the lowly Galilean.

The point to be made is that Christ offered no creed or particular theology. And shortly after his earthly life ended, creeds and theologies began to appear and violence began to be committed in its defense. And always with a theological rationale. In *The City of God* Augustine said, "He to whom authority is delegated . . . is but the sword in the hand of he who uses it . . . [and] is not himself responsible for the death he deals." On that basis Eichmann was innocent. Would you agree that essentially Augustine lays the foundation for the Lutheran position that there is an earthly authority and we shouldn't mess with it? And did Lutheranism pave the way for Hitler's holy war? (Still just asking.) And was not Augustine paving the way to make a moral distinction, not on the basis of conduct, but on the basis of creed? Or belief? But belief is not faith. And faith is not belief. I mentioned earlier those who have not faith, but certitude. Belief is passive. Faith is active. There is but one definition of faith in the New Testament and it has nothing to do with belief, but entirely with action. The one in Hebrews. "Faith is the substance of things hoped for, the evidence of things not seen [Heb. 11:1, KJV]." That is, Abraham going out not knowing whither he went. The Christian going out, not because of some narrow body of doctrine, not because of belief, but in the Spirit of the Way. The way the early builders of the church did not, could not, trust because it wouldn't work in the construction of a mammoth institution. And so, as Hamilton pointed out, there was the gradual trivialization of the church until it had become hardly distinguishable from the society in which it finds itself at a given moment in history.

When Calvin began to formulate a positive conception of the use of Law as a guide to the Christian, even under grace, he was opening once again the floodgate of violence. Dualism, we/they again. Whether it is Calvin and Luther against the Anabaptists, or Pat Robertson, and yes, Patterson, Pressler, and the others against the secular humanists. I asked earlier how these differ. I ask it again. And yes, even throw in Augustine. Are not all of them seeking to make Caesar the adjudicator? Luther's church would find the Anabaptists guilty. The state would execute them. Pat Robertson and the others would find the secular humanists guilty and then turn them over to the state to deal with. How? you ask. Correct them in the public schools. That's how. Can we not all see that to place the Bible in the academic mode, to *permit* it to be taught, let alone to *require* that it be taught, is to deny the very claim that is made: that the Bible is the inspired word of God. And can we not see that to ask the academy to teach our children to pray is to make the academy Lord? "Lord, you teach us to pray," the disciples asked. They did not ask Herod to do it.

Theological preaching? Never thought about it. Now that I have I am convinced that it can only be the living of a life in community, based on faith, not certitude. I don't like the word ministry. It is arrogant, presumptuous, condescending, maybe even imperialistic. I don't have a ministry, I have a life. As to how well I have conducted it, I will leave for God to be the judge, a God about whom I *know* little, but whom I seek to honor.

I conclude with this. A few summers ago our family bookkeeper and financial adviser, who also happens to be my wife of forty-one years, told me that we needed a little money. I asked a friend and neighbor, Waylon Jennings, for a job. After two days on the tour bus unable to figure out exactly what job he had given me, I discovered that I was the one who turned the microwave oven on and off. I was the cook. The band and crew called me Hop Sing, stereotypical perhaps but kinder than some designations that have come my way. Waylon, a dropout a cappella Campbellite from West Texas is not notorious for his religious zeal. His wife, Jessi Colter, is a devout charismatic Christian and sometimes frets about the state of his soul. She asked if, perhaps, maybe I would talk to him sometime. I have always been uncomfortable in the role of an ecclesiastic Peeping Tom, so I said well, perhaps, maybe. About two o'clock one morning on the way from Columbia, South Carolina to Tampa I decided to try it.

"Waylon, what do you believe?" I asked, almost tentatively. There was not the usual shuffling of feet, shifting in the chair, and rubbing of the brow that generally precedes vocal response to such inquiries. Instead he answered quickly.

"Yeah." Way down in his throat. Like he sings.

Now when you're riding a stagecoach from Columbia to Tampa at two in the morning conversations need not be rushed. There was a long pause. "Yeah?" I finally muttered. "Just what the hell is that supposed to mean?"

Apparently he saw no need to hurry the matter along either. As the bus rolled on down America's highway, into the night, we sat in contemplative silence. Then he said, "Uh huh."

Looking back, I suppose that was one of the most profound affirmations of faith I ever heard. "Yeah. Uh huh."

And perhaps one of the greatest bits of theological preaching as well.

CHAPTER 4

What Pastors Can Teach Theologians

David H.C. Read

FOR A LONG TIME THE RELATION BETWEEN PULPIT AND scholar's desk has suggested a one-way flow of traffic that begins in the seminary and, ideally, continues throughout the preacher's career. The lectures, the articles, the commentaries, the products of the theologian's reflections on doctrine, ethics, and ecclesiology are presumed to nourish, stimulate, and discipline the sermons that are dutifully delivered to our theologically untrained and surprisingly uncritical congregations. The preacher thus seems to stand as a kind of dispenser of the pure milk of the Word that is being laboriously extracted at the seminary. To carry a dangerous metaphor a little farther, one might say that those who work at the "Source" may be, and have a right to be, constantly critical of the quality of product eventually delivered to the customers. We are told that it is adulter-

David H.C. Read, D.D., is senior minister at Madison Avenue Presbyterian Church in New York City.

ated, contaminated, soured, made effervescent, or simply transubstantiated into a liquid that is popular, palatable, but bears no resemblance to the pure milk of the Word. To ask a preacher to speak back to the scholarly critics (and I wish there were more of them) then seems like, to use another metaphor, asking an active football player to address an assembly of coaches. It could result in a torrent of criticism of the critics, many statements beginning with the words "It's all very well for you . . ." and snide references to the difference between theory and practice, and perhaps even a citation of the rude epigram of Bernard Shaw: "Those who can, do: those who can't, teach."

That is not the purpose of this chapter. It is written by one who, on more than one occasion, has resisted the appeal of a theological chair, believes that a true preacher *must* be a theologian, and is forever grateful for those whose call has been to theologize full time for the benefit of us all. What I want to do is to reflect on the causes behind the unfortunate divorce that constantly threatens to come between teachers and preachers as servants of the Word, and to offer some suggestions to the seminaries by way of exchange for all I have received, and am receiving from them. My perspective is that of one whose original theological training was in Scotland, France, and Germany, whose preaching ministry can be roughly summarized as fifteen years to Scottish congregations, five years to prisoners of war, and thirty years to New Yorkers.

Let me begin with a question that could be raised in any denomination in any country in the world but is especially acute in the United States today: Why is it that so little of the solid, stimulating, sometimes even exciting, theological work that is being done in the seminaries is seldom reflected in the pulpits—particularly, I am tempted to add, the most popular pulpits of the day? I am well aware of the difficulty for any one of us to make sweeping judgments about our fellow preachers. Perhaps some years of retirement would give me a better opportunity to sample and savor what is being preached around the country. Perhaps our judgments are warped by the fact that those of us with steady pulpit obligations are restricted in our sermon-hearing to the offerings on radio or television—and that would warp anyone's judgment. But from what I hear on vacation, what I read (especially in those subscription services for lazy preachers), and what is reported to me by disappointed parishioners, it seems clear that there is a huge gap between what was absorbed at seminary as to the content of the gospel, and even the ideals of sermon preparation, and what is now being preached. How is it that a man or woman who has been exposed to a first-class theological education and often to excellent homiletical advice should so soon lapse into the trite moralisms, the slick therapy, the cooing illustrations, and the futile exhortations that characterize so much of what is being offered to not only patient, but sometimes enthusiastic congregations today?

One of the obvious reasons for this distressing situation lies in the sheer vitality and activism of the typical American parish. The young ministers, no matter what homiletical ideals they have brought with them from seminary, are immediately sucked into an ecclesiastical machine that demands of them an almost impossible combination of talents—pastor, administrator, educator, editor, budget-builder, counselor, troubleshooter, as well as representative of the church on boards of all kinds (charitable and not so charitable). Of course, this happens to some extent in any Christian parish that is alive in any part of the world, but the American church, with its passion for programs, committees, and efficiency, not to mention the infection of the latest buzzword competitiveness from the secular world, is apt to smother the homiletic ambitions of a new pastor within a couple of years. As he or she returns from a round of meetings and glances at the morrow's calendar, he or she thinks ruefully of the great Dr. Snooks, whom preaching mentors had held up as an example. I mean that mythical character who, besides being a leader in the ecumenical movement, chair of a dozen boards, an indefatigable visitor, fund raiser, and world traveler, spent almost one hour in his study for every minute of sermon he was preparing. My plea to the seminary would be, first, demythologize Dr. Snooks and, second, remember what your first parish was like (if you had one) and be realistic in your expectation, while striving to inculcate a sense of priorities in the pastor's calendar.

That little parenthesis (if you had a parish) brings me straight to another prime cause of the gap between theologian and preacher. I refer to the growing practice of early specialization whereby a seminarian may be encouraged to seek an academic career without ever setting foot in a parish—even someone else's. The tradition in which I was raised held that theologians were to be recruited from the ranks of the parish clergy. There were occasional exceptions, but normally we were aware that the professors who were explicating the doctrines of the Trinity, the documentary mysteries of the Pentateuch, or the Christology of the Prologue to St. John had spent some years expounding the gospel in some country villages or modern suburbs. This fact in no way lessened their impact as theologians, sometimes of worldwide renown, but it did mean that they were living embodiments of the nexus that binds theologian to preacher. In addition, most, as I remember, had a charming and illuminating way of interspersing their profound theological lectures with *obiter dicta* from their parish experience. For instance, one distinguished Old Testament scholar whose theories about the book of Deuteronomy set scholars twittering in distant places would interrupt his dissection of the relevant documents with the remark "The curse of the ministry is laziness." Then I remember Hugh Ross Mackintosh, whose *The Person of Jesus Christ* was at one time required reading in hundreds of seminaries in the English-speaking world, looking up once from his manuscript as he was dealing with one of the harsher interpretations of predestination and saying to us: "Remember, what cannot be preached ought not to be believed." That such *obiter dicta* should keep floating into my mind after more than fifty years suggests to me the importance of this incarnation of the theologian-preacher, and the dangers of any trend toward breeding an ingrown generation of theologians out of touch with the realities of the average parish.

This is not a plea for seminaries to see themselves exclusively as church-related institutions, still less, as "preacher training schools." Historically this double responsibility—toward churches and toward academia—has often been a point of tension, and today in the United States the relative emphasis will depend very much on the stated purpose for which the seminary was founded and the expectations of the governing bodies. A seminary founded and funded for the express purpose of training ministers for a particular denomination is hardly in the same position, or subject to the same pressures, as a divinity school attached to a prestigious university—a remark that is not meant to exclude the possibility of the more-limited institution producing theologians of greater stature in the ecumenical world of historic Christianity than some free-flying products of the university schools. On the continent of Europe, under the influence of the traditional church-state relationship, with its recognition of a national church—whether Roman Catholic, Lutheran, Calvinist, or Episcopalian—

there have been, until recently, few seminaries that saw themselves as merely training schools for the clergy of a particular denomination. Theology ranked with other faculties, such as arts, medicine, and law, as an academic discipline—indeed, as the "Queen of the Sciences," at one time, it outranked them all. It was a study to be pursued for its own sake untrammeled by the requirements of the church either for adherence to doctrinal standards, personal piety, or for practical training in preaching, or the cure of souls. In fact, to this day, it is not unknown for a professor of theology in such an established institution to claim to be an atheist.

The United States has, as we all know, a different history, owing to the famous amendment to the Constitution forbidding the establishment of any church. (How that one plain prohibition has been extrapolated into the arena of Christmas trees on the village green has always been a mystery to this imported Scot.) Theology here found refuge in denominational institutions. Indeed, these were the wombs of many of the great universities, as the study of theology was seen to imply the study of all other disciplines in the academic world. In this way the concept of a seminary as a place where theology could be practiced in its own right, and not just as a handmaid of the pulpit, was preserved. It is not the purpose of this essay to send a message to the theologians that they must view their work as being solely determined by the demand to produce competent preachers. In fact, it is part of the duty of a preacher, when occasion arises, to explain this relative independence of theology to the laity who are inclined to judge the competence of the seminaries they support by the quality of the preachers they produce.

"Relative independence"—the qualifier is surely necessary for any activity of the church, whether in the parish or the seminary, the preacher or the theologian. For all are servants of the Word-made-flesh. If this is kept in mind, some of the tensions between the academic duties of a seminary and its function as a training school for preachers will disappear, for the unifying bond of loyalty to Christ as the Way, the Truth, and the Light will prevent the abuse of the freedom of the gospel in preacher and theologian alike, and each will hear the call to "glorify God and enjoy [God] forever." The scholar immersed in the synoptic problem, or the ramifications of church history is doing that as genuinely as the most eloquent preacher.

I was perhaps fortunate to have attended an institution that was a happy mixture of church seminary and university of divinity. Since the Reformation, theology had been pursued in Scotland's four great universities in close association with all the other academic disciplines. The Disruption of 1843 led to the emergence of a "Free Church," which proceeded to create its own seminaries. These brought the study of theology into much closer contact with the churches, and the teachers were all enlisted from the ranks of the preachers. Adherents of what came to be known as the *Auld Kirk* felt inevitably that these lacked something of the stature of the university professor of divinity, but it soon became evident that the new seminaries were capable of producing theologians of world rank. Happily the Disruption was repaired in 1929, and the national church emerged, representing a great majority of the Christian population. By the time I began my theological studies, New College (the Free Church seminary) had become simultaneously the Faculty of Divinity of Edinburgh University. So, in a sense, we had the benefit of both worlds— the world of theology as an academic discipline to be pursued beyond the horizons of local churches of a particular denomination, and the world of preparation for the work of the ministry with special emphasis on the faithful preaching of the Word.

This little excursus into the tangled field of Scottish ecclesiastical history can perhaps be excused as offering an explanation of the way in which I am sending this message from the pulpit to the seminary desk. I am *not* wanting to say to my theologian friends: "Stop worrying away at your academic specialty; concentrate on giving students a knowledge of the Bible and the ability to interpret it to the average congregation. Give us good preachers and leave all theological speculation to the Germans and the Scots." On the contrary, I thank God that men and women are called with a gift for study and research and an enthusiasm for their specialty to serve as the spiritual and intellectual advance guard of our common task in making the gospel known and confronting the forces of unbelief. What I would suggest, however, is that, just as preachers should acknowledge and celebrate the importance of theology (whenever a preacher says to me, "I'm not a theologian," I want to reply, "Of course you are—you're either a good one or a bad one"), so the theologian should be sensitive to the needs of the churches for effective preachers and be an active member of a particular congregation. Whenever I hear of a theologian who finds it uncomfortable to worship in any church within reach, I am reminded of a remark by Baron Von Hugel, that profound thinker and saint whose writings have nourished so many minds as well as souls, to the effect that he often, on his travels, went to worship in the crudest, ugliest Roman Catholic church in the neighborhood, adorned with the worst excesses of nineteenth-century pietistic art, to remind himself of his membership in the holy, catholic church and the communion of the saints. Even if a teacher has not had the privilege of preaching week by week to fellow Christians, sometimes in the Prot-

95

estant equivalent of Von Hugel's chosen sanctuary, he or she can still be drawn into the fellowship of real human beings, with all their oddities, aspirations, and limitations and be the better for it.

What is needed is more opportunity for fruitful contact and open discussion between theologians and preachers. It is not enough for preachers to attend an occasional conference to listen to lectures on the latest trends. These need to be supplemented by encounters in which a preacher can ask, "Just how would you preach *that?*" or a theologian gently tear a recent sermon to shreds. At all costs we must reverse the dangerous trend toward isolating these two kinds of ministry. If we go that route, we shall find more and more sermons that lack theological backbone, and more and more seminaries in which theologians carry on a kind of incestuous dialogue with their peers in total disregard of the needs of the flocks the preacher knows. Our need for each other as servants of the Word should be becoming more and more obvious. If the teacher withdraws into an academic community to exchange theological papers and enjoy the in-language of his or her specialty, then the preacher may cease to listen to the enriching word from the seminary, and sermons will increasingly be drained of theological content.

There are, of course, many theologians who have the urge to break out of academia and speak to the church at large. A few have had a great impact as preachers and lecturers to the lay world. Since I have been invited to send a message to the seminaries, and not just to applaud the great teacher-preachers, let me risk a comment at this point. What I notice about the theologians who reach large numbers of the general public, either through best-selling books, newspaper articles, or occasional sermons, is not just the refreshing freedom with which they address some controversial question of theology or of politics, but the fact that they often exercise this freedom because they lack the constraints imposed on the parish preacher by the knowledge of the flock. These constraints, let me hasten to add, have nothing to do with the muzzling of the preacher by the sight of Mr. Silas K. Moneybags sitting in the front pew, or the touchy and hypersensitive woman in the row behind. On controversial topics the pastor-preacher knows, as the seminary visitor does not, the good-hearted and genuinely devout people in the pew who are of quite opposite opinions on the topic being addressed. He or she also knows how theological statements that are understood and acceptable in the seminary context can not only be misunderstood, but also be wounding to certain people in the pew. I would plead for a greater sensitivity in the seminary to the pastoral element in all good preaching. Students would then be reminded that they will be conveying biblical truth to a great variety of disciples, or would-be disciples, building up a church in which all may "grow in the grace and knowledge of our Lord and Savior Jesus Christ [2 Pet. 3:18]," and not finding a platform from which to speculate on the latest theological trends or ventilate their political opinions.

This is not to say that the seminarians should avoid reference to all the controversies that make the headlines—"born-again Christians," "glossalalia," "death of God," and the like—or that they should be silent on political issues with moral implications. They should, however, be cautioned against the assumption that the average congregation represents a mass of comfortable prejudices that need to be assaulted at the first opportunity. When the time comes for such an attack it will be infinitely more effective if the preacher has by then won the confidence of the congregation in her or his integrity as an interpreter of the gospel and in pastoral care for her or his people. In the spate of books that appeared about twenty years ago, one could detect a seminary atmosphere that was hostile to the old-style "church on the corner." Bull's-eyes were scored on some of the glaring faults, but there were few words of encouragement for the preachers: their efforts were mostly dismissed as "God-talk" and their liturgies derided in favor of the school of "guitars and balloons." This trend has left little mark on the life of the churches—not, I hope, because we have slipped back into the comfortable ruts beloved by many of the laity, but because there is a new awareness, especially in the younger generation, of the power of the tradition to which we are all heirs. We look to the seminaries as communities where fresh winds are blowing as men and women from the most diverse spiritual roots are open to the life-giving Spirit of God, and are also aware of the dimensions of the holy catholic church, as Paul says, "With deep roots and firm foundations . . . strong to grasp, with all God's people, what is the breadth and length and height and depth of the love of Christ, and to know it, though it is beyond knowledge [Eph. 3:17–19, NEB]."

Here I am touching on a perennial question directed at the theological community. Does the faculty have a responsibility for the spiritual growth of the students, and how can that be fulfilled? Each new generation of students seems concerned about this, especially those who come from home churches marked by a warm, evangelical piety. They are inclined to feel that they have been plunged into a cold bath of intellectualism, sometimes even of cynicism. It is a shock to them to find biblical texts that have nourished their souls subjected to dissection, and doctrines that were accepted with their mothers' milk ruthlessly examined or even rejected. Others, fired by some vision of what ministry can mean in the modern world, find their enthusiasms dampened by the requirement to master the elements of classical theology or to produce a competent piece of exegesis. Still others, who come from a rich liturgical background, are dissatisfied by the meager offerings of chapel worship.

The ramifications of this question are immense. Theological seminaries come in all shapes and sizes, from the most intensely pietistic to the most coldly academic. Students range from flaming evangelists to philosophical dreamers to blazing activists. Teachers may deeply sympathize with the cry for spiritual growth, or may dismiss it as an evasion of the scholarly task. There is no solution to this question that would apply to every seminary in the land. This is an area in which preacher and theologian could confer for our mutual understanding. I would want to say something like this: You have, like the preacher, a responsibility for what used to be called "the cure of souls." Seminarians are all going through a trying and testing period for their Christian faith. There should be no diminishing of your requirement for serious study and a resolute search for truth. Students must learn that seminary training is not a matter of indoctrination to reinforce theological prejudices, but of strenuous examination of the content of the Christian faith and confrontation with both its exponents and opponents in every age. But as members in the Body of Christ, local pastors are called to the pastoral task of helping these students in the Body of Christ; local pastors are called to the pastoral task of helping these men and women through the testing time that a good seminary is bound to offer.

Again, my plea is for a greater unity and cooperation between the seminary, the preacher, and the parish church. Many of us have the joy of watching a succession of our young members respond to the call to the ordained ministry and setting off for seminary. For the average

99

church member this is seen as necessary training, just as other young people may set off to be equipped for the world of medicine, law, or business. Some are under the illusion that such an experience will be spiritually uneventful, a process of learning more about the Bible, confirming one's beliefs, and learning how to conduct services and visit the sick. But we have to recognize that in some quarters, seminaries are viewed with suspicion. A seminary is a place, they believe, where these young Christians will have their faith undermined. Once when I was talking with an old friend of very conservative views genuinely seeking a renewal of the Presbyterian Church, he told me of his concern that our seminaries were not teaching students to believe in the Bible. "In what way?" I asked. "By not taking it literally," he answered. "Like obeying the command 'Thou shalt not suffer a witch to live' [Exod. 22:18, KJV]?" I suggested. "That," he said, "is an exception." Here again, there is a communication breakdown. Many of us preachers have gained enormously from our seminary training with its insights into the nature and composition of the scriptures but have failed to pass this on to congregations. A closer contact between seminary and minister after student days would help to present a truer image of theological education to the members of our churches. Like the preacher, the theologian has a pastoral responsibility.

It is sometimes said that what a pastor has to teach theologians is the art of being understandable by the laity. True, the pastor, by the very nature of the daily round, is in more frequent contact with a broad range of human beings (and conversant with their vocabulary) then the academic. Pastors know—or should know—what words are unknown to their flocks and what words may be misunderstood. They realize the limited capacity of the average layperson for sustained flights of abstract thought. Even when addressing fellow academics, theologians, on occasion, may use the terminology of their discipline without realizing what they are doing. A distinguished professor from another faculty once remarked to me after a university service at Edinburgh, referring to a sermon we had just heard from a brilliant theologian, that "the moment he used the words 'post-exilic Judaism' he lost me." Yet I doubt if this is really the nub of the matter. There are theologians of great erudition and profundity (and sometimes obscurity) whose sermons are direct, clear, and understandable by any congregation. I think, for instance, of Karl Barth, Rudolf Bultmann, Donald Baillie, John Baillie, and Tom Torrance, among others. Obscurity is by no means limited to theologians: some of the most obscure sermons I've heard were delivered by laypeople.

It may even be that theologians who are aware of the relation of their particular discipline to the preaching task are tempted to warn students against importing too much theology into their sermons. Or else they may make no reference, assuming that this sort of thing can be left to the homiletics department. This is where the departmental heresy again raises its ugly head. Potential preachers would gain immensely from an atmosphere in which dogmatics, biblical studies, church history, and other disciplines are naturally associated with the homiletic art. I remember a mind-stretching lecture on the Trinity by Mackintosh at the close of which he remarked: "Don't ever be afraid to preach on this doctrine. You'll be surprised how people will respond." I have found that to be true. Another of my professors, after a thorough critical examination of the relevant Hebrew text, once launched into an impromptu defense of Saul that was one of the most moving sermons I've ever heard. This is the atmosphere that can inspire future preachers and excite them in the task of preparing sermons with theological backbone, without which they will be shortchanging their future congregations.

After hearing a powerful sermon by George Buttrick, at Harvard Memorial Chapel, I remarked to him that every great sermon I had ever heard had something to do with "justification by faith." That is what I mean by "theological backbone." No sensible preacher would throw in that theological phrase expecting a typical congregation today to know what it means. And, of course, I was exaggerating slightly: I must have heard great sermons on other aspects of the faith. But it's not only the fellow preacher who recognizes when a sermon is informed by a solid theology. The laity, too, sense the difference between a sermon that deals with great themes of Christian belief—or at least is clearly inspired by them—and a trickle of moralisms or a ventilation of political prejudices. Some years ago I met by chance a woman who had recently become a member in our church. As we strolled down the avenue I took the opportunity to ask what had led her to this decision. She was a typical New Yorker (if there is such a thing) and a vice-president of a bank. To my surprise she answered at once, "To get some theology." That it was not just *my* theology that appealed is proved by the fact that she is now an ordained minister with her own theology to give backbone to her sermons.

It was the theological weight of their sermons that made the leaders of the Confessional Church in Hitler's Germany the nourishers of a bold resistance. The theology of the Synod of Barmen steeled their sermons. Today, in any totalitarian country, churches cannot live on a diet of fast food such as is happily acceptable in a climate of comfort and safety. When Dietrich Bonhoeffer was at Union Seminary in New York, he took the opportunity to visit many well-known churches and listen to their preachers. I am told that he shocked his fellow students by remarking that the only sermon that really spoke to him was by a local fundamentalist. It, at least, was biblical.

I would tell seminarians that there is no reason a sermon should be intellectually inferior to the content and style of a column by a good journalist, and they owe it to their future congregations not to lead them to expect a told-the-children style with a content that, as one critical layman once said to me, "could be written on the back of a postage stamp, writing large." I would warn them against homiletic treatises that harp on the need for clear structure (introduction; one, two, three, and conclusion) and an abundance of pithy little stories. Excite them with the great themes of the gospel, and they will eventually communicate some of that excitement from the pulpit. Free them from the delusion that there are homiletic tricks that can be learned, and warn them against developing a style and vocabulary that may imprison them for life.

In trying to set down some thoughts that might flow profitably from pastor to theologian, I find that I am fighting the tide of specialization. It is flowing in the parishes where there is a tendency to enclose ministers in their own boxes—preachers, pastors, administrators, evangelists, teachers. As Paul reminds us, there are a variety of gifts, but I'm sure he never envisaged a church led by a series of specialists who had little intercommunication. "Is Christ divided?" as he asked in another context. This tide flows also in the seminaries, where early specialization is, I believe, a temptation for those intent on an academic career. It is flowing also in the courts of church government and denominational administration, where there are "experts" on every conceivable subject. The life of the church today seems often to be fragmented. There are the parishes, the seminaries, and the officials, unkindly known as

103

the "bureaucrats." Sometimes these large groups seem to be pursuing an independent life. If you want to worship, you turn to the parish church. If you want to know what Christians believe today, you turn to the seminaries. If you want to hear pronouncements about current affairs, you turn to the bureaucrats. No wonder the public is confused. And of these three incarnations of the church today perhaps the seminaries may feel the most excluded from power and influence. It need not be so. The pastor must look to the theologian for guidance and inspiration. The bureaucracy must listen to the voice of the parish. The seminary should be aware of the total life of the church in action today. There should be more mutual understanding of the respective roles and a deeper sense of our unity in the service of Christ.

The proliferation of titles describing our specialties is a symbol of this malaise. A minister is a minister is a minister—whether he or she is called bishop, moderator, pulpiteer, professor, executive, or Assistant Deputy Secretary to the Promotion Division of the Board of Christian Education. Central to the vast and scattered organization that is the church in our midst, the work of the theologian reminds us all that we are not an organization competing with a thousand others, but the Body of Christ on earth. If the influence of the seminaries wanes, or they lose touch with the life of the parish or the executive, the cause of Christ is weakened. Fifty years ago the Nazis drove wedges into the competing sections of the church, seeking to capture the bureaucracy and muzzle the preachers. As I noted, it was in the seminaries of the resisting churches that the flame of the gospel was kept alive and theologians nourished preachers and church leaders in the faith of the church—one, holy, catholic, and reformed.

What all this amounts to is an appeal to theologians to be

active in the total life of the church. What I am saying is, "We need you—in the courts and councils of the denominations, both locally and worldwide, in the teaching and evangelism of local churches, in the task of interpreting the gospel to this generation. That there has been too little such collaboration is as much our fault as yours. It is my belief that there is an urgent need for the churches at this time to proclaim the historic faith in terms that make sense to the average educated citizen and reckon with the new horizons, the new religious and ethical dilemmas of our day. The field is open in the matter of popular philosophy and basic beliefs. A glance at religious columns in magazines and newspapers reveals that theological questions are in the air. The churches seem to have surrendered the airwaves to a kind of religioneering that, we would agree, is not truly representative of the Christian faith as we understand it. That is just one sign that there is urgent need for a church that is theologically, intellectually, and spiritually alive. You can help us to become that church."

CHAPTER 5

The Pastor as Public Theologian

Max L. Stackhouse

SOME ASPECTS OF MINISTRY PROPERLY FOCUS ON THE relation of the soul to God. Every pastor knows that the vibrancy of faith depends, in substantial measure, on the quite personal sense of a living relationship between the deepest core of human selfhood and the living God whom Christians have come to know through Jesus Christ. It is a faith relationship that touches heart, spirit, will, and energy. It is the "God Connection," as some of my students call it. According to traditional Christian teaching, the *imago dei* makes this relationship possible; and God's providential will enlivens the relationship by evoking a sense of vocation. The personal "God Connection" means that no one is ever ultimately alone, although we often feel lonely; that no one is without resources, although we often may be

Max L. Stackhouse, Ph.D., is Herbert Gezork Professor of Christian Ethics and Stewardship Studies at Andover Newton Theological School, Newton Centre, Massachusetts.

penniless and exhausted; that no one is without a dignity, although we may feel worthless; and that we have a basis for fidelity, even if much in our feelings and context presses us toward faithlessness.

Different traditions express the vitality of this faith relationship differently—some speak of "knowing Jesus," others of a "feeling of absolute dependence," and still others of experiencing a *mysterium tremendum,* of "forming a spirituality," of developing a "vital prayer life," or of "coming to conviction." In these, and dozens of other formulations, Christians express the inner sense of relation to the living power that is greater than any in the world. This is an indispensable vertical awareness that every pastor must have, and must be able to nurture in others. It is the root of faith. Where it is absent, the pastor burns out, the ministry goes stale, the community of faith loses confidence.

Some aspects of ministry correctly focus on hope. The moments of immediate, faithful awareness of God may seem timeless. Yet even if they pass quickly, they remind us of the eternal, and they empower us both to address moments of hopelessness and to live in disjointed times in expectation. Every current intimation of God has a past that points toward and promises a future when we despair of other evidences. It is one of the key aspects of ministry to cultivate the lore of such moments so that we can gain perspective on what is important in the present and be reminded of the prospects of a promising future. Indeed, our capacities to understand the dynamics of the present and to prepare for the future are as proportional to the amplitude of our memory of the past as they are to our vertical sense of the "God Connection." That is why every seminary prepares people for ministry by requiring substantial familiarity with the history of the Hebrews, of the early church, and of the development of doctrine, ethics, liturgy, and missions over the ages.

Pastors are, among other things, custodians of that memory, recorded in scripture and tradition, for these allow us to encounter and convey the vision of a new heaven and a new earth. The core of the past provides renewed and renewing hope even in the face of suffering and the threats of loss, death, nuclear holocaust, or cosmic entropy. Where this rooted hope is absent, people allow the memories of family, class, or tribal experience to determine their understandings of the present, and anticipate a future that extends no longer than the reading of their wills. Trapped in ghettos of temporal immediacy, people simply endure, without vision. The ends of life are narrow and short.

Still other aspects of ministry correctly demand attention to the horizontal relationships we have with other people. A deep faith and a long hope prompts a wide reach. Reinhold Niebuhr once wrote that "nothing we do, however virtuous, can be accomplished alone. Therefore we are saved by love." Love, like faith and hope, is rooted in the grace of God. It nurtures the capacity to listen to, care for, and share with other people. Love seeks involvement with the neighbor and reaches toward compassionate inclusion of the neglected and the despised. It draws into its scope those whom we could not otherwise stand; it builds enduring bonds of trust and mutuality with all whom it embraces. Love makes every human relationship a co-archy; it resists both domination or subordination. Love invites to service, yet it refuses subservience. This, too, is indispensable to ministry. Where this is absent, leadership becomes managerial, paternalistic, servile, or condescending.

Pastors who already know that faith, hope, and love are radically real are potential members of the communion of the saints—although all of us know ourselves to be less than saintly. But the locus of ministry is not only in the *commu-*

nio sanctorum. It takes place among those specific collections of sinners, housed in quite material buildings, besieged by ideological, material, temporal, and affectional conflicts, that we call "the church." And to deal practically with churches we must add to faith, hope, and love, "wisdom"—the kind of wisdom that is wiser than serpents. It is a kind of prudence that, in the mix and mess of daily life, is able to discern the relative concretions of faith, hope, and love already present and evoke longings for them when they are absent. This entails the craft of ministry, one that structures the common life of worship and witness with the resources at hand, that builds of broken lives a temple to God. Such craftiness demands not only an awareness of the theological virtues, but also a specific kind of graceful shrewdness whereby pastors can see, without becoming cynical, potentialities for faith, hope, and love in the midst of pride, greed, and lust, where they frequently appear.

Ministry, thus, lives in the service of those times and places in which the vertical, the historical, and the horizontal genuinely intersect, and an *ecclesia* is formed. Then we find a lively sense of the holy in the midst of unholy life. We find people touched by a vital spiritual strength; we find horizons expanded by vision, and relationships of grace and equity. When these are organized, celebrated, and acknowledged as gifts of a gracious God, we find that churches become centers of holiness. The wisdom to know how the vertical, the historical, and the horizontal dimensions of holiness can be brought to organizational form, and how they become embodied on earth is also indispensable to ministry.

The Larger World

In one sense, however, these authentic and indispensable dimensions of ministry, and their centers of intersection, are not the end of ministry. They are complicated enough that it is understandable that much of what ministers do is focused only on such matters. But from another perspective these are only the beginning, the point of departure, for faithful and effective ministry. For not only churches, but also civilizations—in other, more complex ways—are concrete embodiments of relative intersections between the vertical, the historical, the horizontal, and the communal dimensions of existence. A public world, which personal spirituality may neglect or flee, is the context of faith. The memories and expectations of peoples, nations, religions, and cultures, which our traditions may not include, are the context of our hope. And neighbors whom we shall never know, but whom we are called to love in impersonal ways, are the context within which our particular affections are bonded. Organized centers of trust, service, and excellence that shape the beliefs, receive the commitments, and preoccupy the people surround the churches we serve.

I am saying nothing that pastors do not already know. We are not oblivious to the fact that when we drive down the street we see not only churches, but homes, schools, shops, factories, police stations, clinics, theaters, and monuments as well. And when we pick up the paper we find sections on business, sports, politics, television, medicine, learning, and law—as well as religion. Do we not, ourselves, turn to the universities when we want education; to the hospitals when we are ill; to the courts to resolve conflicting claims; to the corporations when we want goods or services or jobs; to the concert halls, ball parks, or films when we want entertainment; and to government—even with its instruments of coercion—when we seek the constraint of crime and violence? Such institutions constitute the public world, and those whom we gather in our communities of worship to speak of faith, hope, and love often find their senses of fidelity, purpose, and mutuality in such institutions.

Each of these institutions is constituted by a complex set of trusts, memories, and hopes, by complex networks of affections, and, of course, by communal embodiments of regularized rituals, rites, doctrines, and polities, although they seldom speak of anything theological. Do these institutions not also have, at least potentially, a vertical relation to God, a historical sense of roots and destiny, and a horizontal relation to neighbors near and far? If these public worlds are the larger context of our ministries, we need a public theology to deal with that reality.

We have a name for that which speaks of, invites us to have, and enhances a personal conviction about personal faith: "piety." We also have a name for those normative streams of memory that shape our present and bear promise for the future: "tradition." Still further, we have a name for the kind of bonding, in mutuality, that seeks to secure co-archic human relationships of love: "covenant." And we have a name for the distinctive beliefs that are held by specific religious communities when these are joined: "confessions." All these may be necessary to the formation and preservation of Christian identity; but as my colleague Eleanor McLaughlin pointed out in a recent sermon, identity is frequently nothing more than "individual self-fulfillment at the institutional level . . . [a manifestation of] exclusive individual or tribal values." What we seldom have is a way of critically connecting these to the structures of life in the world, a way of speaking with and to the world, a way of discerning where in the fabric of civilizations the divine may be present, and a way of making the case, in the world, for the significance of that to which we point when we testify to faith, invoke traditions that engender hope,

111

form covenants in love, and make our confessions. Few have a public theology.

The term public theology may be new to some, but it has been around for at least a couple of generations, and it applies to a kind of thinking that has deep roots in Christian history and that intentionally attempts to overcome the relegation to irrelevance the word theology often provokes. Indeed, the case could be made that "theology," in its systematic and critical-reflective senses, did not even appear in Christianity until the confessional foundations of faith, hope, and love, as we see them in the Bible, encountered public worlds beyond its own—in Greek, Roman, and (subsequently) other cultures. In many contexts biblically grounded faith, hope, love, and wisdom have had to make the case, in public discourse, that its deepest concerns were reasonable in the face of, pertinent to, even decisive for, the patterns of thought and structures of civilization in which believers found themselves.

The term is as much a symbol as a concept. That is, it has several levels of meaning that need to be sorted by comparison and contrast with modes of thought to which it is allied but from which it is distinct. Public theology is not, for one thing, "biblical politics," a particular temptation of those branches of Protestantism that take the Reformation doctrine of *sola scriptura* in the direction of bibliolatry. Public theology does not attempt what some Fundamentalists and Liberationists try to do. For example, it does not take the creation story or the references to Armageddon as the basis for political movements to alter government policies in regard to education or nuclear weaponry. Nor does it take the exodus story or the references to the Jubilee as the basis for political movements to alter governmental policies in regard to the Sandinistas or welfare legislation. Public theology takes the witness of scripture more seriously than these selective distortions, for it notes how lopsided such uses of scripture are. Instead, it points out that later scripture uses earlier scripture in a much subtler way, and it reminds us that then is not now, and there is not here.

Political Theology?

Nor is public theology identical with its closest relative, political theology, which both historically and among modern advocates such as Catholic Johannes Metz and Protestant Jurgen Moltmann finds its locus in countries where religion is officially established or, as Frederick Lawrence points out, in lands were religious leadership is part of the unofficial political establishment.[1] Like political theology, public theology does recognize the "crisis of legitimacy" brought about by the attack on traditionally held beliefs at the hands of those modern "masters of suspicion," Nietzsche, Marx, and Freud, and it does recognize that no theology is complete which does not address political responsibilities. But public theology does not begin the approach to the crises of common meaning in modern life through political means. It is instead an attempt to say that political problems are not the primary ones, and that we make an error if we allow the word public to be used in a way that makes all decisions about the common life matters of state.

The differences between public theology and political theology are these: Public theology has a social theory of political life, one that understands religiously rooted metaphysical and moral convictions to be integral to the formation of societies and their constituting institutions, of which one aspect, but not the whole, is necessarily political. Political structures can change and be changed accordingly as they *serve* the other institutions in a civilization, and are obedient to the warranted claims of justice and truth implicit in the governing metaphysical-moral vision, as borne by the nongovernmental institutions. Political theology, in contrast, tends toward a political theory of social life, one that understands political structures to be the *master* of all other institutions in a society. Thus all other institutions are subject to change by the use of political means. Organized religion is tempted to become an instrument of state, or an ideology to seize and guide the state. In short, it is a question of whether the "public" is prior or secondary to the "republic."

At a different level, what is at stake between political theology and public theology is a question of the meaning of the noun that both "public" and "political" modify. What is it that theology offers life and thought beyond the community of worship? Political theology tends to view theology as organized reflection on our faith as we confess it. Theology clarifies dogmatic themes to which a community of believers adheres, and spells out implications for political action. Political theology, in other words, is the modern form of the priestly adviser to princes—in its current radical forms, to pretenders to the thrones of the world.

Public theology, in contrast, is apologetic, not confessional, in approach. It intends to offer to the world not "our confessional perspective," but warranted claims about what is ultimately true and just that pertains to all. It attempts, therefore, to ask: What aspects of the many confessions that religious groups make, including our own, are true and just, as measured by an epistemologically and ethically defensible understanding of what humans can reliably know about truth, justice and God? It is willing to submit the specific contents of its own confessions, of its own faiths, hopes, and loves to public scrutiny, and to

114

engage in those public forms of discourse by which truth and justice are recognized ecumenically and cross-culturally. What theology sets forth, thus, is not in the first instance addressed to political powers, established or anti-establishment, on the basis of "our religion," but to the people through those communities of discourse—scientific, jurisprudential, economic, cultural, technological, etc.— by which people find glimpses of true and just meanings in their lives. When theological claims are made, thus, they are to be filtered through the consciences of the people and linked by them, if by anybody, to political matters.

Several implications follow from this. Insofar as public theology has direct implications for politics, it implies the necessity of "democracy," in the sense that every state or use of political authority is to be limited by the obedience of all state power to publicly discerned first principles. Such a discernment has both cross-cultural and populist elements. It presumes that there are interfaith, constant, and intercultural standards of truth and justice to which every regime must be subject; and it presumes that the people within a given society can sufficiently transcend their own cultural biases to grasp these principles and demand that their own governments be accountable to them. We call these "human rights." Public theology is, thus, not to be confused with any "civil religion," or any "social spirituality" that derives only from the cultural and historical experiences of a given people.[2] Even should these contain universalistic principles, a transcontextual understanding of truth and justice would be required to recognize them.

Public theology has a prophetic streak that invites it to engage and evaluate every religion and every sociocultural context. But unlike those understandings of prophecy that presume a "divine zap" theory of revelation, a public theology presumes that the truth and justice of God can be, in some measure, reliably known through philosophical theology and ethics. What prophetic theology and ethics are about is not privileged, esoteric, or confined to specific confessional identities. In this regard, public theology is closer to certain classic understandings of prophecy that linked it to "natural theology." This can be seen in Augustine, when he linked the biblical tradition to Neoplatonic thought; in Thomas Aquinas, when he used Aristotle and Augustine to join faith and reason; in Calvin, when he spoke of "common" or "general" grace and used Stoic motifs to explicate it; or in Jonathan Edwards, who used Lo ke to speak of a "Consent to Being." None of these, to be sure, end up being philosophical only, for they recognized that metaphysical or moral speculation based only in human reason becomes rudderless. Philosophy requires a God-centeredness to render a genuinely universal sense of truth and justice.

To be sure, such models put an enormous burden on the pastor, one that many would gladly neglect, and that more feel ill-equipped to accept. It is my central contention, however, that the pastor is to be not only one who wisely nurtures Christian faith, hope, and love in specific congregations, but also the philosophical-theologian of universally valid truth and justice in residence among the peoples of God, and to equip the people to discern how and where, *in the world,* the traces of God's truth and justice may be unveiled. Perhaps Whitehead, Tillich, Brunner, Niebuhr, Lonergan, and Panikkar can draw the harvest of modern philosophical, scientific, cultural, social, psychological, and comparative-cultural theories into dialogue with Christian concerns; acknowledge that something of the truth and justice of God may be found in the "secular" modes of understanding; and restate the deepest sensibilities of

Christian claims in ways that allow the world to see their truth, their justice, and their pertinence in the world; but to expect pastors to do the same will be seen by many as simply too much. My argument, however, is that it is precisely this "too much" that must become woven into the fabric of what pastors do.

Some Difficulties

I recognize that this presents difficulties to many modern pastors. One difficulty we have to face is the fact that secularization has shaped us all more profoundly than even our immediate forebears. *Homo religiosus* is, for many in our churches, for some in the ministry, and for more in our culture, intellectually, emotionally, and institutionally segregated from *homo intellectus, homo economicus, homo faber,* and *homo legis.* On the one hand, this has meant that clergy sometimes come to believe that they do not have to think about, systematically study, or be theologically responsible for or to scientific, economic, artistic and technical, or legal structures of modern life. Some, to be sure, preach that *homo religiosus* must become more relevant. But they prescribe only one course: liberation; that is, as Christ overthrows the principalities and powers, so we must act to liberate everything from the prevailing structures of authority.

But the people do not believe us. Clergy proclamations about the horrors of American imperialism or the terrors of multinational corporations are met with the same responses that Catholic laity give to magisterial proclamations about birth control: laity tend to ignore what the pastors say because they do not believe pastors know what they are talking about. They may indulge pastors they love, but they will often try to get them to avoid "politics" and stick to

117

"religious stuff." Current prevalent views of what it means to be relevant and faithful trap the ministry today. If we see "relevance" as "liberation" only, clergy can either "speak out" and be ignored or keep quiet and manicure people's psyches. In either case it means that spiritual, relational, scriptural, and ecclesial matters, which clergy do take seriously, simply become all the more cut off from cultural, social, and civilizational aspects of life wherein the people spend most of their time, energy, and money. "Real life" is therefore set outside the domain of theology and ministry.

A second difficulty we have to face is that today, and in spite of the secularization of many arenas of life, we have no choice but to engage the world's religions in new ways. The religions of the world are not only "long ago and far away," but also in the news every day, among the relatives of people we pastor, and woven into the inchoate beliefs of church members. Magic and most of the ancient heresies are well entrenched in some segments of our churches, as are Hindu views of the soul, Islamic views of the divine dictation of holy writ, Buddhist views of "release," Confucian senses of filial obligation, and pagan views of tribe or clan. Often we cannot recognize them. Max Mueller was surely correct when he said that those who understand only their own religion understand none.

But it is surely also correct that every attempt to encounter other religions introduces the problems of an epistemological, metaphysical, and moral pluralism in new ways. Similarly, much of modern philosophy has become increasingly dedicated to the proposition that there is nothing that can be reliably known about transcendence. Human experience and rationality are on their own; all universalistic claims are historically, psychologically, or linguistically idiosyncratic and perspectival. The foundations of the common life, and of common human understanding, have no warranted bases in, and none for, anything like "God."

These difficulties are reinforced by our daily encounter with the belated fruits of the Enlightenment's rationalistic skepticism about all religious matters, and the Romantic movement's skepticism about both institutional religion and the Enlightenment's rationalism. The echoes of religious skepticism, anti-intellectualism, and anti-institutionalism resonate still in our churches, in our communities, in our human relationships, and in our hearts. As heirs of the Enlightenment and of Romanticism, whether they know it or not, many doubt that faith, hope, love can be connected with truth and justice, in anything like an "objective" sense, in the first place. We have perhaps capitulated too much when we allow the view that between profound faith and profound reason stands a great gulf, that there are no reasonable grounds for being a believer, or that only a faith that is beyond reason can supply insight for life.

One of the greatest temptations of our time is "confessionalism," especially as it tries to be socially relevant on the basis of contextually derived insights. Confessionalism is the view that theology is not a "science" in which there can be any reliable knowledge about God's truth and justice. Rather, it is an expression of personal or group opinion based on what the experience of our social context presents to us, or on what we are acculturated into believing, or on what we choose to believe. Thus what is true or just for some may be quite different for others. Theology then becomes little more than the rationalized clarification of inchoate convictions, and ethics becomes the expressive clarification of values into which we are socialized or for which we arbitrarily decide. Each person, each little group, each corporation and union, each party, each caucus and interest group, and indeed each church asserts what it

119

wants to pursue on the basis of its own confession, often without supplying the warrants as to why anyone not already committed should take us seriously.

Is it not odd that we no longer speak of "Christian persuasion"? The phrase, indeed, sounds quaint today. But I suspect that this signals a profound and dangerous development, especially since we do hear a good bit about who has "power"—clout. Modern intellectual leadership today, including many clergy, has lost confidence in the possibility that we can *know* anything about the most fateful matters for the future of humanity, about what is basic and universally valid in regard to truth and justice, pertinent to the salvation of civilizations as well as souls, and capable of being persuasively argued in the public forums of life. If this is so, clergy have, in fact, no reliable word for the world, no warranted claims to which all should attend, no message for modernity, nothing for those who hear us preach to carry into worlds of work except personal piety, individual hopes, and private affections. For the public world all we have, like every other enclave of special interest, is the possibility of pitting power against power, and interest against interest. But the power of persuasion is not considered to be real power in the ways of the world.

The problem is this: Theology, which is the only thing pastors have to offer the world not already better offered by others, becomes the rhetorically ordered proclamation of what some deeply believe on irrational grounds. But it is something cut off from public discourse, frequently presented in such a way as to suggest that no public warrants for it could be given in the world. Such a view of theology presents at least two problems.

First, in the pluralistic religious world in which we live it is already believed that all religious convictions are a matter of personal or group preference. Some may be into this or that confessing church, others into Sufi meditation, others into Orthodox Judaism, others into the "human potential movement," and still others into Christian pacifism or post-Christian feminism. *All these confessional stances are easily tolerated because they make no basic difference to public life.* Each confessional stance is a curiosity unto itself. "Personally," said a *New Yorker* cartoon figure, "I'm a Zen-Presbyterian."

Second, confessionalism allows the world to wallow in its own pseudorealism. The medical professional is not pressed to struggle with the relation of body to spirit. The legal professional is not prompted to inquire about the relation of substantive to procedural justice. The artist is not called to create or perform under the norm of beauty. The worker and the manager are not called to see their work as a vocation from God, but can be satisfied with a job or a career. The historian, the scientist, and the journalist can compile facts and correlate data without attentiveness to meaning and value. And public figures can worry about public image, but ignore public virtue. All may, in their personal lives, embrace one or another confession and be "good people," but the fundamental claims of faith about what is ultimately true and just do not form or inform the way "real life" is conducted.

Today we might better take our models from those Christians in such places as India, China, Indonesia, and Korea, who, as tiny minorities, are struggling to make the case as to how and why certain Christian theological understandings of God's truth and justice might well be valid foundations for the transformations of ancient personal loyalties and of ancient, if now rapidly modernizing, cultures. These are among the pastoral theologians of our day whom we should emulate. They refuse to be merely confessional; they refuse merely to oppose Christianity to the structures

121

of complex civilizations; and they refuse to limit the meanings of faith to "private" matters. Instead, they seek to discern where in their cultures the universal living God is present, to state persuasively, in dialogue with non-Christians, something of the nature of truth and justice by which the common life might be transformed. And in the process they find both that many discover the foundations of faith, hope, and love in new ways, and that their own confessions are altered in wider directions.

The Agenda for Pastors

We are badly in need of a new *apologia* for normative public theology and ethics in our day, one that can make the case for the fact that Christian theology and ethics are sciences—art/sciences perhaps but sciences nonetheless—by which we can know that what we teach and preach in churches and enact in the world about faith, hope, and love involves a reliable approximation to the truth and justice of God.

I have referred several times to "truth and justice." I recognize that this is not the most frequent juxtaposition of terms used by clergy today. More frequent are references to "praxis." Indeed, if there is one sacred arrow in the quiver of those who believe themselves to be in the battle for a relevant contemporary theology, one supposed to be the bench mark for ministry today, it is "praxis." The term, however, is not a simple one, and it is, in some ways, one of the most abstract terms of contemporary thought. Orlando Costas, a noted Latin liberationist, is among those who have tried to give it precise definition. He defines "praxis" in this way: "action that provokes reflection and is corrected by it, and reflection that is verified by efficacious action."[3]

It is clear that everything in this definition begins and

ends with action. Action is to provoke reflection, and reflection is to be verified by action. But the key normative term in this definition is "efficacious." It is, in other words, another way of speaking about that prudent wisdom which knows how things work, how things get done in the world, and what it takes to be effective. Many in the clergy need prompting in this direction, but I will not focus on this point at this time for the simple reason that I do not think that "praxis" is what the church needs most. I fear that the appeal to "praxis" begs several questions: What is the basis of the initiating action? How do we know what actions will provoke the kind of reflection that does not become merely utilitarian or "technical," or even Machiavellian?

It is possible to answer such questions by saying "the gospel." But that is just the point: "praxis" requires a prior theory of the meanings, the purposes, and the principles that ought to guide actions and the kinds of reflection that, when prompted by action, guide action in valid directions. Further, reflection is itself an action, and the questions we confront today have to do with what actions and what reflections are worth doing. By what standards, to what end, under what principles? We must have, in other words, standards by which it knows whether there are any guidelines by which we can give substance to "efficaciousness," or else we end up with a mere actionism.

Still further, it is a serious question as to what people mean by "the gospel." It may be that what we want to put into practice is faith, hope, and love. But, as I have already argued, these stand today only on confessional grounds, often disconnected from the wider civilizational and intellectual contexts that we must today encounter with new depths. Not a few versions of what the gospel is are quite unbelievable. Further, we want to know whether that in which we have faith, that by which we hope, and that through which we order our love is valid, especially since much of the world does not believe that what we do in the churches on these points has any foundations.

I turn to the key terms "truth" and "justice" to suggest those standards by which we guide our faith, our hope, and our loves—indeed, by which we wisely shape our "praxis." A public theology takes these as touchstones of the logos of God from the foundations of creation. They are, therefore, the foundations for a warranted praxiology. No God and no claims about God, no confessions about God and no appeals to have faith, hope, or love in God, no actions for God or reflections to guide action are believable unless they are true and just.

These two criteria have a particular pertinence in our world for reasons that Costas suggests. Two groups particularly need to know that there is a basis for Christian faith, hope, and love.[4] One group consists of those who have passed through the skepticism, suspicion, and doubt of the post-Enlightenment period. Many exposed to modern science, technology, sociology, psychology, anthropology, and philosophies have come to the conclusion that most of what "religion" talks about is a matter of personal preference, for which no public warrants can be given. Religion is thus relegated to private feelings, and has value primarily, as Robert Bellah has taught us, only insofar as it meets the needs of our therapeutic or managerial individualism.[5] Many, if not most, of the leaders of intellectual, professional, and cultural life, and not the least, the media, have such a view. They are quite willing to have clergy cultivate the private virtues, massage people's feelings, and repeat a church confession, so long as no claims about their "truth" are made. Religious matters are "newsworthy" only when they are absurd (as Oral Roberts' claims seem to be) or when they are likely to have direct political fallout (as when the Christians, Jews, and Muslims shoot at one another in Lebanon). All claims about God or humanity or sin or grace or salvation are understood to be cultural opinions or psychologically variant perspectives that some people may choose to believe. As Timothy Jackson has demonstrated, however, this means that nothing can ever be taken as really, objectively, basically holy, right, or good—or, for that matter, "perverse," "heretical," "abominable," or "wrong."[6] Not only theology suffers, but also philosophy, jurisprudence, education, literature, and human rights everywhere.

I wonder, in this connection, how many clergy basically believe that what we are called to uphold to the world is indispensable to the salvation of the world; that societies collapse without a metaphysical vision that engages, deepens, broadens, and transforms its basic theoretic foundations; and that the gospel becomes most clear and compelling when it wrestles with, converts, and gives new coherence to that which is beyond itself. To put it in stronger terms, modern society has contracted a metaphysical disease. The somewhat deceptive, relative health of many institutions in modern civilization derives from the fact that many of them were formed in periods informed by a theologically rooted consciousness of God's truth and justice as it wrestled with the hard questions of civilizational formation. We are living on the capital of earlier public theologies. But that same relative health obscures the metaphysical emptiness of the present as well as the facts that no civilization has ever managed to exist without continued guidance from a credible metaphysical-moral vision, and that our society, deciding that one is either dispensable or impossible, has relegated all theological matters to the marginality of private opinion.

The people in our churches sense this, I believe; and

that is why many "liberals" seek a "new spirituality" (which is not infrequently an old gnosticism), and why many "evangelicals" are tempted to fundamentalism (which is often a bibliolatry). Both seek a metaphysical vision that neither contemporary society nor confessional theology supplies. And if the people are not offered a public theology, nonsense or fanaticism will fill the vacuum.

The second group that needs to know that there is some foundation for Christian faith, hope, and love consists of those who have suffered dehumanization through slavery, colonialism, patriarchy, exploitation, or powerlessness. These seem to have much less of an "intellectual" or "metaphysical" problem than a "social" or "ethical" problem, for which justice is the only answer. It does little good to speak of faith, hope, and love with these folks, unless these virtues are connected to those public institutional transformations that make justice a possibility. Public theology, political theology, and liberation theology are agreed on this point.

But just at this point we face secondary problems. Our society has become unsure about what justice is, indeed of whether justice is at all. And many in the global community doubt that there are cross-cultural standards of justice—which means that people of one context cannot persuade others, from other contexts, of the righteousness of their protests against injustice, and that those outside a particular context can have nothing to offer those within that specific context.

Further, many of the analyses of the causes of injustice set forth on behalf of the dispossessed, the poor, and the oppressed today derive from modes of social analysis that, themselves, are very doubtful as to whether there is, or could be, anything like an objective standard of justice. The notion that there is, say some people, merely echoes of idealistic and intellectualistic approaches to reality, which were the artifacts of elites to control others and that need to be overthrown. In the attempt to overthrow such "abstractions" they turn to "praxis" understandings of social reality with renewed vigor. But these seldom contain, as we have seen, any governing definitions of either justice or truth to give praxis a logos. The truth of the situations they encounter, they say, are contextual injustice, and cannot be understood by anyone who is not part of the acting-reflecting community, trying to be efficacious.[7] And at this point one sees a new, now secular post-Enlightenment confessionalism, rooted in contextual specificities, that does not, and cannot, claim that the core of what they are about is fundamentally just. The accounts of how cultures, communities, societies, and civilizations work in relation to basic theological and ethical norms, which derive from these analyses, do not convince anyone not part of the enclave in the first place. And that is, in part, why "solidarity with the oppressed" has become a "preferential option."

It is not, I want to argue from the standpoint of a public theology, a preferential option. It is a matter of the truth and justice of God that is at stake. Claims about truth that are not linked with justice, and claims about justice that are not linked to truth, are not of God. And neither Christianity nor modern civilizations are served well in the long run by intellectuals who, because they do not believe in God, also doubt truth and justice, or by activists who believe in God but have no way of speaking about the truth and justice of God beyond the dynamics of their contextual confessions.

Perhaps it is now clear why I think that pastors today must not only continue to cultivate the virtues of Christian faith, hope, and love, with wisdom, in the contexts of our communities of worship, but also become, to do so in a convincing and genuine way, "public theologians" willing to take on the additional burdens of recovering and recasting the fundamental notions of truth and justice in the larger domain of public discourse. Our task becomes one that is constantly shuttling from the centers of Christian piety, tradition, and covenant to the periphery of apologetic encounter with the largest, most pervasive metaphysical-moral questions facing humanity.

We have some models in this regard. Reinhold Niebuhr's *Nature and Destiny of Man* remains a classic for our times. So do key works composed by pastors: I invite you to read again Martin Luther King's *Letter from a Birmingham Jail*, paying particular attention to the kinds of arguments he marshals to address the church and the public. Look also to the Roman Catholic Pastoral Letter on the nuclear problem. And note the irony that it is today the "learned clergy" among nonfundamentalist evangelicals and "Christian Unitarians" where questions of apologetics are most eagerly studied.[8]

And how can we who are not Niebuhrs or Kings or bishops or pastor-scholars begin to become public theologians? I think we have to begin with one area of study beyond our ordinary range of reading, thought, and reflection. It may be law, or medical ethics, or philosophy, or some dimension of the natural or social sciences. Or it may be one of the world's religions. And this we have to master, all the while inquiring as to how the deepest, broadest theological orientations we can find speak to, inform, transform, and integrate with the traces of truth and justice we find there. But more important, we have to ask what it is that theology has to say that would and could be persuasive to those who think, live, and work in this way—indeed whether we have anything important to say to that arena of discourse. I suspect that we will find the classic theological doctrines—such as Creation, Fall, Salvation, Trinity, and Sacrament—can and do connect with what we discover and provide resources to the field we have chosen that are not otherwise present. And once we have begun to see how to make the connections in one field, we will see analogues to others. Then we need to preach and teach on these matters, equipping the people to become theologians of God's truth and agents of God's justice in the worlds in which they live, empowered by a faith, hope, and love that have foundations.

I am well aware that this proposal would demand, in the long run, also the reform of theological education, the redefinition of the nature and character of the message we have to deliver, and the reorganization of what pastors read and do daily. It also demands that we look deeper into the traces of God's justice and truth that may be residually present in jurisprudence, economic theory, and behavior and in academic, artistic, and technological life; but I see no alternative if not only souls, but also civilizations are to be saved.

Notes

Introduction

1. Previous titles in this series edited by Earl E. Shelp and Ronald H. Sunderland are *The Pastor as Prophet* (1985), *The Pastor as Servant* (1986), and *The Pastor as Priest* (1987).
2. Cf. John Macquarrie, *Principles of Christian Theology*, 2nd ed. (New York: Charles Scribner's Sons, 1977), p. 1.
3. Ibid., pp. 14, 20.

Chapter 1. The Pastor as Theologian

1. Gerard Manley Hopkins, "The Habit of Perfection," *Poems of Gerard Manley Hopkins*, ed. W.H. Gardiner (New York: Oxford University Press, 1948), p. 47.
2. "The Litany" (concluding prayer), *The Book of Common Prayer*.
3. Cf. Thomas Sheehan, *The First Coming* (New York: Random House, 1987).
4. Cf. Carl Becker, *The Heavenly City of the Eighteenth Century Philosophers* (New Haven, CT: Yale University Press, 1932).
5. Cf. Robert Nisbet, *History of the Idea of Progress* (New York: Basic Books, 1980).
6. Cf. two different but equally useful current probings of this crucial point: F.W. Dillistone, *The Power of Symbols in Religion and Culture* (London: SCM, 1986), and Janet Martin Soskice, *Metaphor and Religious Language* (New York: Oxford University Press, 1985).

7. But notice the saint's blithe unrealism about his expectations of his prospective readers: "The purpose we have set before us in this work is to convey the things that belong to the Christian religion in a style serviceable for the training of beginners *(incipientum)*." Thomas Aquinas, "Prologus," *Summa Theologiae*, Blackfriars edition (New York: McGraw-Hill, 1964), vol. 1, p. 3.

Chapter 2. Black Theology and Pastoral Ministry

1. W.E.B. DuBois, *The Souls of Black Folk* (Greenwich, CT: Fawcett Publications, 1961), p. 23.
2. Martin Luther King Jr., *Where Do We Go from Here? Chaos or Community* (New York: Harper & Row, 1967), p. 134.
3. Gayraud S. Wilmore, "Cultural Renewal: The Vocational Responsibility of the Black Church," unpublished paper read at the annual meeting of the Society for the Study of Black Religion, October 1985.
4. In July 1964 a rally called in New York by the Congress of Racial Equality developed into a clash with police in which twelve officers and nineteen marchers were injured. For several days the police fought blacks in Harlem and the Bedford-Stuyvesant section of Brooklyn. Blacks fought back with Molotov cocktails, bricks, and bottles and the police with gunfire. Many people were injured. See *Report of the National Advisory Commission on Civil Disorders* (New York: E.P. Dutton & Co., 1968), p. 36.
5. The first official statement on black theology is found in Gayraud S. Wilmore and James H. Cone, eds., *Black Theology: A Documentary History, 1966–1979* (Maryknoll, NY: Orbis Books, 1979), p. 100.
6. *Presbyterian Outlook*, May 25, 1981, p. 9.
7. James M. Washington, ed., *A Testament of Hope: The Essential Writings of Martin Luther King, Jr.* (San Francisco: Harper & Row, 1986), p. 279.
8. On the pneumatological basis of black theology, see Theo Witvliet, *The Way of the Black Messiah: The Hermeneutical Challenge of Black Theology as a Theology of Liberation* (Oak Park, IL: Meyer-Stone, 1987).

9. James H. Cone, *Black Theology and Black Power* (New York: Seabury Press, 1969).

10. Joseph A. Johnson Jr., *Proclamation Theology* (Shreveport, LA: Fourth District Press, 1978).

11. Cecil W. Cone, *The Identity Crisis in Black Theology* (Nashville: African Methodist Episcopal Church, 1975), and Henry H. Mitchell, *Black Belief: Folk Beliefs of Blacks in America and West Africa* (New York: Harper & Row, 1975).

12. Henry H. Mitchell and Nicholas C. Lewter, *Soul Theology: The Heart of American Black Culture* (San Francisco: Harper & Row, 1986). See p. 11 and the statement on the dust jacket.

13. William H. Grier and Price M. Cobbs, *Black Rage* (New York: Basic Books, 1968), p. 22.

14. Ibid., pp. 196–97.

15. Thomas C. Oden, *Pastoral Theology: Essentials of Ministry* (San Francisco: Harper & Row, 1983), p. x.

16. I first heard this challenge from the Rev. Raul Suarez, a leading Cuban theologian of liberation, at a conference in Havana in 1986 with the faculty of New York Theological Seminary. Suarez defines liberation theology in Cuba as a pastoral theology.

17. James H. Cone, *Speaking the Truth: Ecumenism, Liberation, and Black Theology* (Grand Rapids, MI: Wm. B. Eerdmans Publishing Co., 1986), pp. 31–32.

18. Sydney E. Ahlstrom, *A Religious History of the American People* (New Haven, CT: Yale University Press, 1972), pp. 12–13.

19. *Atlanta Constitution*, March 3, 1987, p. A4.

20. Witvliet, p. 88.

21. Cone, *Black Theology and Black Power*, p. 151.

22. Witvliet, p. 170.

23. James H. Cone, *For My People: Black Theology and the Black Church* (Maryknoll, NY: Orbis Books, 1984), p. 205.

24. Ibid., pp. 206–7.

Chapter 3. Values and Hazards of Theological Preaching

1. Edith Hamilton, *Witness to the Truth* (New York: W.W. Norton, 1948), p. 205.

Chapter 5. The Pastor as Public Theologian

1. Frederick Lawrence, "Political Theology," *Encyclopedia of Religion* 11 (New York: Macmillan Publishing Co., 1986), pp. 404–8. See also Max L. Stackhouse, "Politics and Religion," ibid., pp. 408–23.
2. I have dealt with these at some length in *Creeds, Society, and Human Rights* (Grand Rapids, MI: Wm. B. Eerdmans Publishing Co., 1984).
3. Orlando Costas, "A Vision for the Future," unpublished manuscript presented at the American Baptist Seminary of the West, September 1986, p. 13.
4. Ibid., p. 7.
5. Cf., Robert Bellah, *Habits of the Heart* (Berkeley: University of California Press, 1984).
6. Timothy Jackson, "Ethics, Abominations, and Liberations," address to the Society of Christian Ethics, January 1987, pp. 6f. and passim.
7. Max L. Stackhouse, "Contextualization and Theological Education," *Theological Education*, Autumn 1986, pp. 67–84.
8. See, for example, C. Stephen Evans, *Philosophy of Religion* (Downers Grove, IL: InterVarsity Press, 1985), and James Luther Adams, *The Prophethood of All Believers*, ed. G.K. Beach (Boston: Beacon Press, 1986).

DUE